Tolkien
and the Silmarils

৯৯

Tolkien
and the Silmarils

Randel Helms

HOUGHTON MIFFLIN COMPANY · 1981

Library of Congress Cataloging in Publication Data

Helms, Randel.
    Tolkien and the Silmarils.

    Includes bibliographical references and index.
    1. Tolkien, John Ronald Reuel, 1892–1973.
Silmarillion. I. Title.
PR6039.0'32S533   823'.912   80-20346
ISBN 0-395-29469-X

Printed in the United States of America

P 10 9 8 7 6 5 4 3 2 1

The author is grateful to Houghton Mifflin Company for permission to quote from the published works of J. R. R. Tolkien and from *Tolkien: A Biography* by Humphrey Carpenter.

To my parents,
Loyce V. Helms and Vernell Helms

Contents

Introduction:
"The Silmarils are in my heart"

ϑ☙

The Silmarillion is J. R. R. Tolkien's most complex and challenging work; this book attempts to provide a way through its difficulties with an account of its origins, sources, and themes, and of the relationship it bears to the author's other writings. *The Silmarillion* seems to have been Tolkien's favorite undertaking; its writing covered a span of fifty years and its narrative underlies both *The Hobbit* and *The Lord of the Rings*, providing them with episodes, themes, history, and languages. Indeed *The Silmarillion* competed with *The Lord of the Rings* for Tolkien's time and attention in the late 1930s, very nearly overcoming, blotting out, the story of the One Ring before it was well begun. We should remember that *The Lord of the Rings* was an afterthought, an accident of the success of *The Hobbit*, summoned into existence initially as an act of will rather than creative necessity when Stanley Unwin, Tolkien's publisher, wrote calling for "another book about the Hobbit." [1] But on receiving Unwin's letter Tolkien felt at first that stories about hobbits were ancillary to his real creative work. Writing in response, he declared that though "it is plain . . . a sequel or successor to *The Hobbit* is called for," his imagination at the time was leading him far elsewhere — into *The Silmarillion*, a work

Unwin's editorial readers had just seen in an unfinished state
and declared unsuitable:

> But I am sure you will sympathize when I say that the
> construction of elaborate and consistent mythology (and
> two languages) rather occupies the mind, and the Sil-
> marils are in my heart. So that goodness knows what will
> happen. Mr Baggins began as a comic tale among con-
> ventional Grimm's fairy-tale dwarves, and got drawn into
> the edge of it — so that even Sauron the terrible peeped
> over the edge. And what more can hobbits do? (Dec. 16,
> 1937 — Carpenter, p. 185)

Though his rational sense of the limitations of hobbits left out
of account the depth of their meaning to his imagination, for
the moment at least he was right — hobbits *were* ancillary to
what was really in his mind, the story of the Silmarils, and the
initial effort at a sequel to *The Hobbit* was halfhearted, break-
ing off for a while at the end of the work's first chapter, "A
Long-expected Party," with the not very fruitful notion that
Bilbo disappeared because he "had not got any money or jewels
left" and had decided to go off to hunt for more (Carpenter,
p. 185). A few months after this unpromising beginning and
more false starts — Bilbo's nephew was first called "Bingo Baggins" — Tolkien wrote to Allen & Unwin that "The sequel to
The Hobbit has remained where it stopped. It has lost my fa-
vour, and I have no idea what to do with it" (July 24, 1938 —
Carpenter, p. 187). Some thirty years later Tolkien looked back
on this time (with a rather faulty memory), declaring again that
in late 1937 his heart was really with the Silmarils, though every-
one else seemed to want hobbits; the Foreword to the second
edition of *The Lord of the Rings* says of the work that

> It was begun soon after *The Hobbit* was written and be-
> fore its publication in 1937; but I did not go on with this
> sequel, for I wished first to complete and set in order the

mythology and legends of the Elder days, which had then been taking shape for some years. I desired to do this for my own satisfaction, and I had little hope that other people would be interested in this work, especially since it was primarily linguistic in inspiration and was begun in order to provide the necessary background of 'history' for Elvish tongues.[2]

The evidence, however, is clear that Tolkien did *not* begin writing *The Lord of the Rings* before the publication of *The Hobbit* on September 21, 1937, for he had written to Unwin promising to give "thought and attention" to his publisher's suggestion about a sequel to the story for children on December 16, 1937, and to Charles Furth at Allen & Unwin on December 19, saying that he had just finished a first chapter for the new book. But though he is wrong about the date, and wrong about the interest others would eventually take in *The Silmarillion*, Tolkien gives us here an important insight into the origins of the work. It began with language, with words, the Elvish Quenya and Sindarin tongues he had been amusing himself with inventing since his youth. He created the languages, and then felt called upon to make a world in which they could exist, a world suited to their particular sounds and imaginative effects:

> *A Elbereth Gilthoniel*
> *silivren penna míriel*
> *o Menel aglar elenath!*
> *Na-chaered palan-díriel*
> *o galadhremmin ennorath,*
> *Fanuilos, le linnathon*
> *nef aear, sí nef aearon!* [3] (I, 250)

Perhaps it is not quite correct to say that Tolkien felt called upon to create a world for his languages: *enchanted* is a better word. For this is a song in Sindarin about Elbereth Star-Kindler, one of the very songs Frodo heard at Rivendell, with the same effect on him that such language appears to have had on Tolkien:

> the beauty of the melodies and the interwoven words in the Elven-tongue ... held him in a spell ... Almost it seemed that the words took shape, and visions of far lands and bright things that he had never yet imagined opened out before him; and the firelit hall became like a golden mist above seas of foam that sighed upon the margins of the world. Then the enchantment became more and more dreamlike, until he felt that an endless river of swelling gold and silver was flowing over him (I, 245–6).

Frodo is rapt in what Tolkien elsewhere calls "the elvish craft, Enchantment," and so was Tolkien, though he himself invented both the elves and their craft. For as he wrote in "On Fairy-Stories," "Enchantment produces a Secondary World into which both designer and spectator can enter, to the satisfaction of their senses while they are inside." [4] Enchanted by his own creations, he had no choice but to give them all a local habitation and a name, a Secondary World at which he worked from 1917 until his death.

The following chapters will trace the growth and culmination of that labor of more than fifty years in *The Silmarillion*. Chapter I examines the origins of Tolkien's Secondary World, which he called Middle-earth (after the *middangeard* of Old English poetry), from its beginnings with Tolkien's fascination with a pair of lines in an Anglo-Saxon poem (encountered in 1913) to the completion of the three earliest tales (in the year 1917) of what was to become *The Silmarillion*.

Those three stories of 1917 ("The Fall of Gondolin," "Of Túrin Turambar," and "Of Beren and Lúthien") formed part of what Tolkien had originally planned as a volume to be called "The Book of Lost Tales," but as he wrote them, they seemed to summon, almost unbidden, something larger, a Secondary World, and called forth new themes, awoke new influences — chief among them the Bible, John Milton, and the *Elder Edda*. My second chapter traces Tolkien's use of those major themes and sources in *The Silmarillion*, the work that "The Book of Lost Tales" became. The third chapter is a study of the specific source and structure of *Quenta Silmarillion*; the fourth does the same for *Akallabêth*. Chapter Five looks at the ways in which *The Silmarillion* underlies both *The Hobbit* and *The Lord of the Rings*.

Tolkien declared in his Foreword to *The Lord of the Rings* that his purpose was to write a "really long story that would hold the attention of readers, amuse them, delight them, and at times maybe excite them or move them." *The Lord of the Rings* succeeds admirably in that aim and requires little help from a commentator. I think the same cannot be said with entire truth of *The Silmarillion*; it is a book in need of a second reading, a book — such is my hope — made more available and enjoyable with the aid of something like the present study.

Tolkien
and the Silmarils

I

Eala Earendel:
The Origins of *The Silmarillion*

ဦ

The Silmarillion began with a word, with language compelling and strange to the ear: *Earendel*. From the word grew a tale, and then a world for its setting. "Names," Tolkien has said, "always generate a story in my mind" [1]; he encountered this name as an undergraduate at Oxford, studying Old English. There in 1913 he read the *Crist* of Cynewulf and found two lines that would not leave his thoughts:

> *Eala Earendel engla beorhtast*
> *ofer middangeard monnum sended.*

"Hail Earendel, angel brightest/ over middle-earth unto men sent." Tolkien would have known by this time that *Earendel* in Anglo-Saxon means "shining light" and refers to the planet Venus, but in association with "middle-earth" and "angel" the word seemed to reverberate with a deeper meaning. Looking back on this time as an older man he wrote that encountering the lines "I felt a curious thrill, as if something had stirred in me, half wakened from sleep. There was something very remote and strange and beautiful behind those words, if I could grasp it, far beyond ancient English" (Carpenter, p. 64). Soon the young Tolkien, imagination already deeply stirred, encountered Earendel again, this time not directly as a star-angel, but as the *originator* of a star. As part of his B.A. program in English philology, he undertook a study of Old Norse and its literature, reading the *Prose Edda* of Snorri Sturluson. There he came across the story of Aurvandil, whose name is the Old Norse cognate for the Anglo-Saxon *Earendel* (and referring, like its cousin, to the planet Venus). In the tale, the god Thor fought the giant Hrungnir, killing him; but in the battle, the giant flung his whetstone in an attempt to block Thor's hammer. The stone shattered and part of it pierced Thor's head. The god hurried to the sybil Groa, who "recited spells over Thor until the hone worked loose." As Groa chanted, Thor attempted to please her with the good news that he had rescued "her husband Aurvandil from giantland," carrying him on his back in a basket. One of Aurvandil's toes, however, "had stuck out of the basket and been frozen, so Thor had broken it off and thrown it up into the sky and made of it the star called Aurvandil's Toe." [2] A grotesque and hardly promising tale, but Tolkien was to remember it when Eärendil (and something connected with him) enters heaven as a star.

At about this time, Tolkien's undergraduate research might well have brought him across the old Germanic story of Erentil, or Orendel (the Old High German cognate of *Earendel*), whom Jakob Grimm, in his *Teutonic Mythology*, describes as the "first of all heroes," a mariner who suffers shipwreck, takes shelter with the fisherman Eisen, and later weds "Breide, the fairest of women." [3] Here then are the bones of the story of Eärendil in *The Silmarillion*: a mariner-hero, wed to a beautiful woman, who becomes a star. Tolkien's imagination had only to blend them together and create a new thing, and it did within less than a year. In the summer of 1914 he composed what turned out to be the earliest version of the *Lay of Eärendil*, in the form of a not very promising narrative poem about the sky-voyager Earendel, who seems equivalent to the morning and evening star:

> Earendel sprang up from the Ocean's cup
> In the gloom of the mid-world's rim;
> From the door of Night as a ray of light
> Leapt over the twilight brim,
> And launching his bark like a silver spark
> From the golden-fading sand
> Down the sunlit breath of Day's fiery death
> He sped from Westerland.

According to Carpenter the "succeeding verses describe the star-ship's voyage across the firmament, a progress that continues until the morning light blots out all sight of it" (Carpenter, p. 71). These metrically unsophisticated lines give us the beginnings of Eärendil's role as the morning star, but they lack any mention of the Silmarils or of a broader, deeper Secondary World; these are yet three or four years in the future.

Gradually the story of Earendel fleshed itself out in Tolkien's mind, as his adolescent desire to become a narrative poet grew apace, chiefly under the inspiration of William Morris, whom he began avidly reading in 1913. Such works as *The Earthly Paradise, The House of the Wolfings,* and Morris' translation of *The Völsunga Saga* set Tolkien's young imagination on fire, especially *The Earthly Paradise,* which tells of a group of mariners who set sail in search of the land that grants its inhabitants immortality (a source, ultimately, of part of *Akallabêth*); after years of toil and wandering they arrive at an unidentified land and hear a series of mythological tales, one of which is called "The Land East of the Sun and West of the Moon." Inspired by these, Tolkien continued work on the "Lay of Earendel," composing as part of it a poem called "The Shores of Faery," about a land lying "West of the Moon, East of the Sun," to which Earendel sails. There he sees "towers white and still:/ Beyond Taníquetil/ In Valinor," among which stand "Two Trees" that bear the golden apples of the sun and silver apples of the moon (Carpenter, p. 76). Here stand the first hints

of the larger Secondary World of *The Silmarillion,* though
there remain some major gaps in the plan, not least the Silmarils
themselves.

Thus by 1915 (at age twenty-three) Tolkien has reached
this point: though writing derivative and undistinguished verses,
he is gradually working his way toward a conception of a
Secondary World, a "Faery" realm called Valinor, visited by
the mariner Earendel. He needed now to grow up, as man and
as writer, before bringing to fruition what he had begun; the
next two years saw this growth. Tolkien graduated from Oxford in 1915, married Edith Bratt and enlisted in the Lanca-
shire Fusiliers in 1916, and went on to see action and terrible
destruction in the Battle of the Somme, in which twenty thousand Allied troops perished on the first day alone. Becoming ill
with trench fever, he was sent home to recuperate, a process
filling most of 1917. During that lengthy recovery, he learned
that he had, besides Edith, only one close friend left alive; all
the rest had died in the trenches in France. Love, war, death: the
end of childhood.

The fighting and the loss of his friends affected Tolkien
deeply, touching his imagination in ways he probably did not
understand intellectually for years. One major effect was to
strengthen his desire to write fantasy, to live, imaginatively, in
a Secondary World, the world of *The Silmarillion.* As he wrote
in 1938, "A real taste for fairy-stories was wakened by philology
on the threshold of manhood, and quickened to full life by
War." [4] Until the publication of *The Silmarillion,* the meaning
of this sentence was not entirely clear; it seemed to refer to *The
Lord of the Rings,* a work not even begun until twenty years
after the war ended. But now it is evident that the remark refers
to the origins of his first great work, not to be published until
nearly forty years after this sentence in "On Fairy-Stories" was
written. Tolkien's love of philology gave him Earendel and thus
the beginnings of *The Silmarillion;* the effects of the war were

the next step. The first story he wrote in hospital during re-
cuperation from trench fever was the original version of "The
Fall of Gondolin," his account of the great defeat in the Sixth
Battle of the Wars of Beleriand. The time of writing is no
accident. The tale describes a disastrous lost battle, from which
Eärendil is carried away to a safe stronghold, there to meet the
woman he comes to love, and thence to go on later to Valinor,
home of the elves. The same, of course, was true of Tolkien:
carried away from the disastrous lost Battle of the Somme, back
to safety in England, to Edith, and recovery in hospital, where
he entered his Secondary World, peopled by the elves of his
imagination. It has been remarked that alone of the stories Tolkien wrote in 1917 (which included the original versions of "Of
Beren and Lúthien" and "Of Túrin Turambar"), "The Fall of
Gondolin" employs no literary sources (Carpenter, p. 92); it
grew from Tolkien's own imagination and experience of disaster.
But that story served as a release; once his imagination was freed
into fairy-story, he turned to a combination of personal and
literary memory to continue his first extended work. Tolkien
wanted at first to call his new undertaking "The Book of Lost
Tales," and to model it after *The Earthly Paradise* of William
Morris. Few books have begun with larger hopes; it was to be
massive, comprehensive, mythological. As an older man, Tolkien
looked back upon his youthful plans somewhat ruefully:

> once upon a time (my crest has long since fallen) I had
> a mind to make a body of more or less connected legend,
> ranging from the large and cosmogonic to the level of
> romantic fairy-story ... I would draw some of the great
> tales in fullness, and many only placed in the scheme, and
> sketched ... Absurd (Carpenter, pp. 89–90).

Yet despite the grandiose plans, "The Book of Lost Tales" was
still derivative in structure; like its model, it was to tell of a
group of mariners who land on a strange shore and hear a series

of legendary tales. "Tolkien's voyager," says Carpenter, "was
called Eriol, a name that is explained as meaning 'One who
dreams alone'" (Carpenter, p. 90). A stranded sailor, listening
to a set of tall tales: not the most promising of literary devices,
nor one conducive to tight, coherent structure or large themes
about an entire created world. But as we shall see, the tales grew
in the telling; by the end of 1917 they had overcome their original setting and *The Silmarillion* was under way. His experiences
with Edith and the war solidified his youthful reading and en-
thusiasms, gradually freeing his imagination from its juvenile
derivative state and setting loose his first masterpiece, the second
"Lost Tale" of 1917, "Of Túrin Turambar." We see Tolkien in
this work learning to outgrow an influence, transform a source,
developing a crude medieval tale into a larger and finer thing.
His source was the story of Kullervo in *The Kalevala,* a poem
he had found fascinating since his youth. Already at age twenty-
two Tolkien had attempted a version of that story in his own
words, in a prose-and-verse form modeled after Morris' *House
of the Wolfings,* but the effort remained unfinished (Carpenter,
p. 73). The story bubbled slowly in the back of his mind, waiting to attach itself to a larger, more comprehensive theme. Indeed it is a tale that begs to be transformed: Kullervo as he
appears in the Finnish epic is little more than a lustful and
murderous bully. Returning once from a journey, he notices
a young girl, a "golden maid" on snowshoes, and accosts her:

> Come, sweet maiden, to my snow sledge,
> In my fur-robes rest and linger.

Not surprisingly, she refuses. Later, Kullervo sees another girl,
and approaches her with the same words. She too knows better.
Finding a third maiden, he changes his tactics, forcing her
bodily into his sled. She pleads for release:

> Loose me from thy magic power,
> Let me leave at once thy presence.

Instead he tempts her with his hoard of wealth:

> Shows the maiden gold and silver,
> Shows her silken wraps of beauty,
> Silken hose with golden borders.
> Golden belts with silver buckles,
> Jewelry that dims her vision,
> Blunts the conscience of the virgin.[5]

Thus sorely tempted, she relents, spending the night with Kullervo in his fur-robes. Next morning they belatedly exchange names, only to find to their horror that they are both the children of Kalervo, full brother and sister. Overcome by the revelation, the girl drowns herself and Kullervo falls upon his sword. Scarcely an uplifting story, though certainly a fascinating one; Tolkien's second attempt to deal with it found him a more mature writer, able to transform its more sordid elements and relate them to the larger theme then growing in his mind. First, he changes the character of his Kullervo figure, whom he names Túrin. Like Kullervo, Tolkien's hero was born after a great battle in which his father was killed. Both youths grow up in the house of a noble relative, Untamo in *Kalevala*, Thingol in *Silmarillion*. In the home of his foster father, Kullervo signally fails to ingratiate himself; set to nursing, he kills the infant; set to chopping wood, he destroys a forest; to building a fence, he constructs a vast impassable barrier. Disgusted, Untamo sells Kullervo to Ilmarinen, who puts him to work as a cowherd. But he soon quarrels with Ilmarinen's wife, and in revenge turns all the cattle into bears and wolves, who then kill her. Kullervo flees from his master's wrath, an act Tolkien borrows for his story. Túrin likewise quarrels with and kills a member of his master's household and must flee; but Tolkien's version of Kullervo appears as a much more noble figure, not one to injure without cause. His first violent deed comes in response to a grievous insult. Saeros, another member of Thingol's court, had "long begrudged to Túrin the honour he had received as Thingol's fosterson." One day he taunts Túrin, who has returned from battle with worn and war-damaged gear. Túrin in great anger "took up a drinking vessel, and cast it at Saeros; and he was grievously hurt." Later the vengeful Saeros ambushes Túrin, only to be himself killed. Túrin flees and becomes an outlaw, as does Kullervo on the death of Ilmarinen's wife. Later Kullervo returns to his own people, there to seduce his sister.

Túrin's love for *his* sister must be told with a different basis and different motivations. Tolkien's effort to transform the more sordid elements of the Kullervo story gave him, as it turned out, a better handle on a major theme and character in the developing *Silmarillion*: the role of Morgoth. In the first of the "Lost Tales," "The Fall of Gondolin," Morgoth was eager, for reasons not yet clear perhaps even to Tolkien himself, to destroy the elvish stronghold and anyone associated with it. But Tolkien's hero Eärendil, still a boy, was rescued from the doomed city and spirited away to the coastlands, from which he would someday make his all-important voyage to Valinor and bring about the destruction of Morgoth. That tale, however, was yet several years in the future (Tolkien had imagined Eärendil's voyage to Valinor but not its purpose or result). In the meantime he needed to establish the character and machinations of Morgoth. The first "Lost Tale" showed him the originator of the evil deed of Maeglin, the betrayer of Gondolin — Morgoth will work through the moral ruin of others. The second "Lost Tale" shows a similar method of evil, the ruin of brother and sister. Tolkien was able to add even further depth and complexity to his version of the Kullervo figure by blending him with Sigurd, the hero of *The Volsunga Saga* and the *Elder*

Edda, and with Beowulf, and by introducing a version of the dragons fought by these heroes.

Use of the dragon allows Tolkien to change the motive for the hero's incest. Kullervo's sin with his sister comes from little more than lust, and even appears as somewhat comical; after all, she is the third girl he has tried to entice into his fancy vehicle, and then he only succeeds by a combination of force and bribery. Tolkien employs not bribery but the dragon spell, and thus excuses both Nienor, Túrin's sister, and his hero, who had never seen her before; the dragon

> laid a spell of utter darkness and forgetfulness upon her, so that she could remember nothing that had ever befallen her, nor her own name.[6]

Later, when her company of protectors was attacked by orcs, Nienor fled

> as in a madness of fear, swifter than a deer, and tore off all her clothing as she ran, until she was naked (p. 219).

Túrin Turambar finds her thus and pities her, and soon "all her heart was given" to him (p. 220). They marry, and in the course of time she is with child. Having succeeded thus far, the dragon Glaurung ponders new evil. He attacks the land, calling forth Túrin. Since Tolkien has with Glaurung introduced his version of the dragons of *Beowulf* and the *Eddas,* he proceeds to make Túrin like the heroes of those works. Like Beowulf, he volunteers to go alone against the dragon:

> he counselled them that it was vain to go against Glaurung with all their force, for only by cunning and good fortune could they defeat him. He offered therefore to seek the dragon on the borders of the land and bade the rest of the people to remain at Ephel Brandir.

Túrin kills Glaurung in a scene modeled directly after Sigurd's slaying of Fafnir in the *Elder Edda*, though Tolkien makes his hero's courage even finer than Sigurd's. Sigurth (as he is called in the *Edda*) digs a great trench across the dragon's path, and lies in wait:

> when Fafnir crawled over the trench, then Sigurth thrust his sword into his body to the heart.[7]

So Sigurth's courage is in some part guile. Tolkien changes the scene:

> the dragon lay at Cabed-en-Aras, where the river ran in a deep and narrow gorge that a hunted deer might over-leap ... [Túrin] purposed to creep down at dusk and descend into the ravine under night, and cross over the wild water; and then to climb up the further cliff, and so come to the dragon beneath his guard (p. 221).

This desperately courageous plan terrifies Túrin's companion Dorlas: "he dared not attempt the perilous crossing, but drew back and lurked in the woods." Sigurth likewise has a cowardly companion, Regin, who had "gone to a distance while Sigurth fought Fafnir, and came back while Sigurth was wiping the blood from his sword." Enraged by such cowardice, he "hewed off Regin's head."[8] Tolkien, on the other hand, ennobles his hero in that Túrin does not kill the fearful Dorlas, leaving that to Brandir, who slays him in the woods (p. 224).

Having ennobled his hero, added complexity to his motivation, and introduced richer elements from *Beowulf* and the *Edda*, Tolkien felt free to return to a close repetition of his source in the closing of the tale. First, however, he makes the revelation of the incest much more striking than in the *Kalavela*. It is Glaurung himself, with his dying words, who declares Nienor's blood relationship to her husband:

"Hail, Nienor, daughter of Húrin. We meet again ere the end. I give thee joy that thou hast found thy brother at last . . . Túrin son of Húrin! But the worst of all his deeds thou shalt feel in thyself."

Then Glaurung died, and the veil of his malice was taken from her, and she remembered all the days of her life.

"Distraught with horror and anguish," and thinking herself "happy to be dead," she flings herself over the brink of Cabed-en-Aras and disappears into the river, like her matrix, the sister of Kullervo. The revelation of the incest in the *Kalevala*, on the other hand, is much less dramatic and psychologically interesting. It may even be seen as somewhat comical, for Kullervo and his sister ask each other's names only after spending "the night in merry-making." Learning Kullervo's identity, the young woman leaps into a nearby river. Kullervo too ends his own life in a scene faithfully imitated by Tolkien:

> Kullervoinen, wicked wizard,
> Grasps the handle of his broadsword,
> Asks the blade this simple question:
> "Tell me, O my blade of honor,
> Dost thou wish to drink my life-blood,
> Drink the blood of Kullervoinen?"
> Then his trusty sword makes answer,
> Well divining his intentions:
> "Why should I not drink thy life-blood,
> Blood of guilty Kullervoinen,
> Since you feast upon the worthy,
> Drink the life-blood of the righteous?" [9]

So Kullervo falls upon his sword and dies. Túrin likewise

> drew forth his sword, that now alone remained to him of all his possessions, and he said: "Hail, Gurthang! No lord or loyalty dost thou know, save the hand that wieldeth

thee. From no blood wilt thou shrink. Wilt thou therefore take Túrin Turambar, wilt thou slay me swiftly?"
And from the blade rang a cold voice in answer: "Yea,
I will drink thy blood gladly, that so I may forget the
blood of Beleg my master, and the blood of Brandir slain
unjustly. I will slay thee swiftly" (p. 225).

Túrin too falls upon his sword.

With "Of Túrin Turambar" "The Book of Lost Tales"
had begun to characterize a deeply wicked antagonist — Morgoth — but had as yet no adequate protagonist; Túrin dies, and
in "The Fall of Gondolin" Eärendil appears only as a boy. The
third "Lost Tale" of 1917 remedied that need, while at the same
time showing Tolkien's exploitation of his newly won mastery
in combining literary influence with his own experience to produce not derivative juvenilia, as formerly, but a full-fledged
masterpiece, "Of Beren and Lúthien." Not only is this work the
finest of the "Lost Tales" of 1917, it so transcended and over-
whelmed the structural limitations of his first plans that Tolkien
became aware he must devise some new basis for his mythological stories, some large and adequate form to comprehend where
his imagination was leading him: a Secondary World was beginning to grow and could no longer be contained in a set of
"overheard" tales. "The Book of Lost Tales" must before long
give way to *The Silmarillion*; not only can we see this beginning
to happen in "Of Beren and Lúthien," we can even watch Tolkien groping toward his new title.

"Of Beren and Lúthien" is the first of a surprisingly large
number of stories in which Tolkien presents a man meeting,
becoming enchanted by, and loving a female elf. There are four
of such meetings in his works (and one exactly parallel in which
a male elf meets a female Maia). The kind of setting and the
way of meeting are uniform, a set pattern in Tolkien's mind
that comes, first, from a traditional scene in mythology and
literature, but that was fixed in Tolkien's heart by his own ex-

perience. The meeting of Beren and Lúthien is for him the archetype:

> Wandering in the summer in the woods of Neldoreth he came upon Lúthien, daughter of Thingol and Melian, at a time of evening under moonrise, as she danced upon the unfading grass in the glades beside Esgalduin. Then all memory of his pain departed from him, and he fell into an enchantment (p. 165).

The pattern continues in the meeting of Thingol and Melian:

> he came alone to the starlit wood of Nan Elmoth, and there suddenly he heard the song of nightingales. Then an enchantment fell on him, and he stood still; and afar off beyond the voices of the *lómelindi* he heard the voice of Melian, and it filled all his heart with wonder and desire. He forgot then utterly all his people and all the purposes of his mind (p. 55).

A generation later, in the "Tale of Aragorn and Arwen," Tolkien finds the same pattern in his imagination:

> Aragorn walked alone in the woods, and his heart was high within him; and he sang, for he was full of hope and the world was fair. And suddenly even as he sang he saw a maiden walking on a greensward among the white stems of the birches; and he halted amazed . . .
>
> For Aragorn had been singing a part of the Lay of Lúthien which tells of the meeting of Lúthien and Beren in the forest of Neldoreth. And behold! there Lúthien walked before his eyes in Rivendell (III, 338).

We need not seek far to find the source of this pattern of meeting; the pattern itself is ancient, widespread in northern European mythology: any man who comes upon elves in the forest is likely to find himself enchanted, if not worse. Such meetings and enchantments are likewise traditional in literature; probably the best known example in English — and one beloved by Tol-

kien, who quotes it in "On Fairy-Stories" — is the ballad of
Thomas Rymer:

> True Thomas lay o'er yond grassy bank,
> And he beheld a ladie gay,
> A ladie that was brisk and bold,
> Come riding o'er the fernie brae.

The lady tells him that she is the "queen of fair Elfland," and
that "ye maun go wi me now Thomas." He is enchanted away
to her land of Faery, losing account, like Thingol, of all in the
ordinary world:

> And till seven years were past and gone
> True Thomas on earth was never seen.[10]

But that enchanting meetings with elvish ladies are traditional
in literature does not explain the hold of such scenes on Tolkien's imagination; it was his own experience that fixed it there.
Tolkien loved his own Lúthien.

Anyone who stands before the long home of Ronald and
Edith Tolkien will see this carved on their stone: *Edith Mary
Tolkien, Lúthien, 1889–1971. John Ronald Reuel Tolkien, Beren,
1892–1973.* Tolkien's love for Edith lies behind Beren's for
Lúthien and may be a chief reason why "Of Beren and Lúthien"
is the most profound and moving of the tales in *The Silmarillion,*
the one in which he invested the greatest care and craft, filling
it with more detail, more emotional force, than any other story.

Fifty years after completing the tale, Tolkien wrote to
his son Christopher of their recently deceased wife and mother:
"She was (and she knew she was) my Lúthien." Like Beren's
long-delayed marriage to Lúthien, so Tolkien and Edith's union
marked the end of a lengthy period of separation and unhappi-
ness; in the same letter quoted above, Tolkien spoke of the
"dreadful sufferings of our childhoods, from which we rescued
one another, but could not wholly heal wounds that later often

proved disabling" (Carpenter, pp. 97–98). Beren's meeting with Lúthien in a woodland glade, and all those other man-elf meetings in the years to come, were the products of Tolkien's own meetings with Edith. During his leave from the trenches in 1917, he and Edith often went for walks in the countryside. Near Roos they

> found a small wood with an undergrowth of hemlock, and there they wandered. Ronald recalled of Edith as she was at this time: "Her hair was raven, her skin clear, her eyes bright, and she could sing — and dance" (Carpenter, p. 97).

Thus a central scene in *The Silmarillion* and the "Tale of Aragorn and Arwen."

Even after the glade meeting, the personal parallels continue. Being elvish, Lúthien is of course much older than Beren; Edith Bratt was three years older than Tolkien. And being elvish, Lúthien was "different" from the mortal Beren; Edith, Protestant Anglican, was likewise different from the Roman Catholic Tolkien. Because she was different, and older, and because Tolkien was still a teen-ager when they fell in love, his guardian (for he was an orphan like Beren) Father Francis Morgan stepped between them, as his concept of duty required, insisting that Tolkien not see her again, as Lúthien's father Thingol saw to it that the young lovers would be (he hoped) forever parted. So until his majority, Tolkien obeyed Father Francis, waiting until his quest of manhood was complete. This intriguing set of personal parallels is matched by an equally intriguing set of literary parallels, for "Of Beren and Lúthien" found its chief written source in the "Culwch and Olwen" section of the Welsh national tale, *The Mabinogion*. We can in fact observe a broadening and deepening of Tolkien's literary skills during the course of 1917, as he learned the knack of a creative blending of personal experience and literary influence.

The first of the "Lost Tales," "The Fall of Gondolin," presents a kind of symbolically heightened autobiography and employs no literary sources; it is probably the least interesting of the tales of that year. The second, "Of Túrin Turambar," is a greatly improved revision of a Medieval poem, but it seems in some places curiously flat, lacking emotional power. But the third, "Of Beren and Lúthien," is a wonderfully rich combination of autobiographical reference and revised medieval tale — in this case, *The Mabinogion.*

In the Welsh story, the hero Culwch is put under an enchantment by his wicked stepmother:

> "I will swear a destiny upon thee, that thy side shall never strike against woman till thou win Olwen the daughter of Ysbaddaden Chief Giant." The boy coloured, and love of the maiden entered into every limb of him.[11]

Beren too "fell into an enchantment" with love of Lúthien (p. 165). Like Olwen the unreachable daughter of a great giant, Lúthien is the unattainable child of the great king Thingol. In each story the hero approaches (after perilous passages) the father and asks for the hand of the daughter, who already loves him in return, and in each the father knows that her marriage to the young hero will mean his own doom: Ysbaddaden grasps, says Olwen, that "he shall live only until I go with a husband," [12] just as Thingol learns from Melian that "it is ill for you, whether Beren fail in his errand, or achieve it. For you have doomed either your daughter, or yourself" (p. 168). Knowing this and not wishing the marriage of his daughter, each father requires the young suitor to perform an impossible quest. Ysbaddaden declares that "When I myself have gotten that which I shall name to thee, then thou shalt get my daughter." [13] Among other unattainable treasures, he demands

> the cup of Llwr son of Llwyrion ... thou shalt not have it of his own free will, nor canst thou compel him ... The

ment must have come in the year or two preceding 1920. We can, I think, trace his thinking in the matter. Beren's quest object had loomed up as the center of the now-burgeoning story, the source of all that rankled in Middle-earth. Tolkien's discovery of the importance and history of this object had come through the influence of the quest story in *The Mabinogion*, a work whose title comes from the Welsh plural form *mabinogi*, meaning "youths" or "heroes." If *The Mabinogion* is then the story of the mabinogi, the heroes of Wales, his tale, thought Tolkien, is the story of the *Silmarilli*, a Quenya plural form meaning "jewels of silima": thus *The Silmarillion*.

hamper of the Gwyddnew Long-shank ... He will give it to no one of his own free will, nor canst thou compel him ... The horn of Gwlgawd Goddodin ... He will not give it of his own free will ... The harp of Tiertu ... The birds of Rhiannon ... The Cauldron of Diwrnach ... The tusk of Ysgithryrwyn Chief Boar ... The blood of the Black Witch ... the bottles of Gwddolyn the Dwarf ...

and so on for eight pages. Ysbaddaden wants to be quite sure Culwch will never succeed! Tolkien reduces this complex and even comically long list of impossible deeds to but one, gaining a good deal of power and intensity for his story in the process: "Bring to me in your hand," says Thingol to Beren, "a Silmaril from Morgoth's crown; and then, if she will, Lúthien may set her hand in yours" (p. 167). In both tales, the daughter loves and encourages the hero, and in both the young men enlist the aid of a great king: Culwch goes to Arthur, Beren to Finrod Felagund. In both works the hero carries an identifying ring, Culwch one recognized by Custennin's wife (guardian of Ysbaddaden's castle), Beren a ring given to his father by Finrod, one recognized by the guardians of Nargothrond. In both tales, a great dog aids the hero in his quest: "Cafall, Arthur's own dog," helps in the killing of Ysgithrywyn Chief Boar, and Huan, greatest of the hounds of the Valar, performs mighty acts in aid of Beren's quest, not least the killing of the great werewolf of Morgoth, Carcharoth. In both works a magical blade must be captured from a powerful person to bring about the success of the quest. In *The Mabinogion*, only the sword of the giant Wrnach can slay him, and it must be brought to Ysbaddaden from the giant, who will never give it up; in *The Silmarillion*, the knife Angrist, which can cut through iron, must be captured from Fëanor's son Curufin, so that Beren may use it to cut a Silmaril from the iron crown of Morgoth. And finally, of course, in both works the quest succeeds, the object is won. The power Tolkien gained for his tale by mastering the combination of literary influence and personal memory served him throughout the rest of his now-growing work.

"Of Beren and Lúthien" provided Tolkien's final imaginative release into the rich Secondary World of *The Silmarillion*. What had begun with *Eala Earendel engla beorhtast* found its meaning in the star-shine of the Silmarils. "Bring to me in your hand a Silmaril," says Thingol to Beren. But what was a Silmaril? Tolkien's imagination told him that Beren's quest object was related to Earendel shining in heaven. But how? *The Silmarillion*, as opposed to the "Book of Lost Tales," began here, with the quest object and its imaginative ramifications. That this should be so is not unusual in the history of myth and literature. Remember that Beren's quest began with Tolkien's imaginative association of Edith, for whom he had to perform a quest of maturation, with Lúthien, the final object of Beren's quest. The next step, nearly inevitable, was the imaginative association of Lúthien/Edith with the precious jewel, the Silmaril itself:

> Bring to me in your hand a Silmaril from Morgoth's crown; and then, if she will, Lúthien may set her hand in yours. Then you shall have my jewel; and though the fate of Arda lie within the Silmarils, yet you shall hold me generous (p. 167) —

lovely Lúthien, herself a jewel greater even than those "three great jewels ... Like the crystal of diamonds" (p. 67). To the mythological imagination, such jewels are virtually identical, different aspects of the same thing. "The mythological goal," according to Erich Neumann, is "almost always the virgin, the captive, or more generally, the 'treasure hard to attain' ... In the earliest mythologies ... as well as in fairy tale, legend and poetry, gold and precious stones, but particularly diamonds ... are all symbols of the treasure." [14]

It is with such objects of desire, objects of endless imagi-

native ramification, that truly sub-creative labor b Secondary World is born:

> Anyone inheriting the fantastic device o guage can say *the green sun*. Many can th picture it. But that is not enough — tho ready be a more potent thing than man sketch" or "transcript of life" that receive
>
> To make a Secondary World inside sun will be credible, commanding Secor probably require labour and thought, a demand a special skill, a kind of elvish

A Secondary World begins with a *green sun* ing to the imagination. Tolkien's green sur jewel in Morgoth's crown. How did it get asked himself next. Morgoth stole it, cam whom? Who made it? Who made the M nature of the world they lived in? Such qu must have flooded into Tolkien's mind in Tales" were giving way to *Silmarillion*. his imagination did work this way, back quest-object to maker to meaning, for w to himself early in the invention of Boo *Rings*, at a time when he was still not s book was to be about: "The Ring: w mancer? Not very dangerous, when But it exacts its penalty. You must e (Carpenter, p. 186).

Having outgrown, through Silmaril as filtered through *The M* structure, the work needed a new ti and meanings, its new Secondary know exactly when Tolkien chan

> hamper of the Gwyddnew Long-shank ... He will give it
> to no one of his own free will, nor canst thou compel him
> ... The horn of Gwlgawd Goddodin ... He will not give
> it of his own free will ... The harp of Tiertu ... The
> birds of Rhiannon ... The Cauldron of Diwrnach ... The
> tusk of Ysgithryrwyn Chief Boar ... The blood of the
> Black Witch ... the bottles of Gwddolyn the Dwarf ...

and so on for eight pages. Ysbaddaden wants to be quite sure Culwch will never succeed! Tolkien reduces this complex and even comically long list of impossible deeds to but one, gaining a good deal of power and intensity for his story in the process: "Bring to me in your hand," says Thingol to Beren, "a Silmaril from Morgoth's crown; and then, if she will, Lúthien may set her hand in yours" (p. 167). In both tales, the daughter loves and encourages the hero, and in both the young men enlist the aid of a great king: Culwch goes to Arthur, Beren to Finrod Felagund. In both works the hero carries an identifying ring, Culwch one recognized by Custennin's wife (guardian of Ysbaddaden's castle), Beren a ring given to his father by Finrod, one recognized by the guardians of Nargothrond. In both tales, a great dog aids the hero in his quest: "Cafall, Arthur's own dog," helps in the killing of Ysgithrywyn Chief Boar, and Huan, greatest of the hounds of the Valar, performs mighty acts in aid of Beren's quest, not least the killing of the great werewolf of Morgoth, Carcharoth. In both works a magical blade must be captured from a powerful person to bring about the success of the quest. In *The Mabinogion*, only the sword of the giant Wrnach can slay him, and it must be brought to Ysbaddaden from the giant, who will never give it up; in *The Silmarillion*, the knife Angrist, which can cut through iron, must be captured from Fëanor's son Curufin, so that Beren may use it to cut a Silmaril from the iron crown of Morgoth. And finally, of course, in both works the quest succeeds, the object is won. The power Tolkien gained for his tale by mastering the combination of literary influence and personal memory served him throughout the rest of his now-growing work.

"Of Beren and Lúthien" provided Tolkien's final imaginative release into the rich Secondary World of *The Silmarillion*. What had begun with *Eala Earendel engla beorhtast* found its meaning in the star-shine of the Silmarils. "Bring to me in your hand a Silmaril," says Thingol to Beren. But what was a Silmaril? Tolkien's imagination told him that Beren's quest object was related to Earendel shining in heaven. But how? *The Silmarillion*, as opposed to the "Book of Lost Tales," began here, with the quest object and its imaginative ramifications. That this should be so is not unusual in the history of myth and literature. Remember that Beren's quest began with Tolkien's imaginative association of Edith, for whom he had to perform a quest of maturation, with Lúthien, the final object of Beren's quest. The next step, nearly inevitable, was the imaginative association of Lúthien/Edith with the precious jewel, the Silmaril itself:

> Bring to me in your hand a Silmaril from Morgoth's crown; and then, if she will, Lúthien may set her hand in yours. Then you shall have my jewel; and though the fate of Arda lie within the Silmarils, yet you shall hold me generous (p. 167) —

lovely Lúthien, herself a jewel greater even than those "three great jewels... Like the crystal of diamonds" (p. 67). To the mythological imagination, such jewels are virtually identical, different aspects of the same thing. "The mythological goal," according to Erich Neumann, is "almost always the virgin, the captive, or more generally, the 'treasure hard to attain'... In the earliest mythologies... as well as in fairy tale, legend and poetry, gold and precious stones, but particularly diamonds... are all symbols of the treasure." [14]

It is with such objects of desire, objects of endless imagi-

native ramification, that truly sub-creative labor begins and a
Secondary World is born:

> Anyone inheriting the fantastic device of human lan-
> guage can say *the green sun.* Many can then imagine or
> picture it. But that is not enough — though it may al-
> ready be a more potent thing than many a "thumbnail
> sketch" or "transcript of life" that receives literary praise.
>   To make a Secondary World inside which the green
> sun will be credible, commanding Secondary Belief, will
> probably require labour and thought, and will certainly
> demand a special skill, a kind of elvish craft.[15]

A Secondary World begins with a *green sun,* an object vivify-
ing to the imagination. Tolkien's green sun was a Silmaril, a
jewel in Morgoth's crown. How did it get there? he must have
asked himself next. Morgoth stole it, came the answer. From
whom? Who made it? Who made the Maker? What was the
nature of the world they lived in? Such questions as these surely
must have flooded into Tolkien's mind in 1917 and 1918 as "Lost
Tales" were giving way to *Silmarillion.* Indeed we know that
his imagination did work this way, backward as it were, from
quest-object to maker to meaning, for we have a note he wrote
to himself early in the invention of Book I of *The Lord of the
Rings,* at a time when he was still not sure what the new hobbit
book was to be about: "The Ring: whence its origin? Necromancer? Not very dangerous, when used for good purpose.
But it exacts its penalty. You must either lose it, or *yourself*"
(Carpenter, p. 186).

   Having outgrown, through Beren and his quest of the
Silmaril as filtered through *The Mabinogion,* its "Lost Tales"
structure, the work needed a new title matching its new powers
and meanings, its new Secondary World vastness. We can't
know exactly when Tolkien changed the title, but the develop-

ment must have come in the year or two preceding 1920. We
can, I think, trace his thinking in the matter. Beren's quest object had loomed up as the center of the now-burgeoning story,
the source of all that rankled in Middle-earth. Tolkien's discovery of the importance and history of this object had come
through the influence of the quest story in *The Mabinogion*,
a work whose title comes from the Welsh plural form *mabinogi*,
meaning "youths" or "heroes." If *The Mabinogion* is then the
story of the mabinogi, the heroes of Wales, his tale, thought
Tolkien, is the story of the *Silmarilli*, a Quenya plural form
meaning "jewels of silima": thus *The Silmarillion*.

II

The Major Themes:
Mythology in *The Silmarillion*

ह

TOLKIEN had his green sun by 1917; now he needed a Secondary
World inside which that green sun would be credible, com-
manding what he called Secondary Belief. "I had a mind," he
wrote later of his wish at this time, "to make a body of more
or less connected legend, ranging from the large and cosmogonic
to the level of romantic fairy-story" (Carpenter, p. 89). Such a
desire — to create one's own world — is at the heart of all mythologies; a desire, said Tolkien, divinely implanted, clear sign
of the spark illuming us all. In a little doctrinal poem he wrote
to C. S. Lewis in the 1930s while trying to convert Lewis to
Christianity (and succeeding), Tolkien named the source of this
desire:

> Although now long estranged,
> Man is not wholly lost nor wholly changed.
> Dis-graced he may be, yet is not de-throned,
> and keeps the rags of lordship once he owned:
> Man, Sub-creator, the refracted Light
> through whom is splintered from a single White
> to many hues, and endlessly combined
> in living shapes that move from mind to mind.
> Though all the crannies of the world we filled
> with Elves and Goblins, though we dared to build

> Gods and their houses out of dark and light,
> and sowed the seed of dragons — 'twas our right
> (used or misused). That right has not decayed:
> we make still by the law in which we're made.[1]

"We make in our measure and in our derivative mode, because we are made: and not only made, but made in the image and likeness of a Maker." [2]

So Tolkien became as a god, knowing good and evil and writing his own Book of Genesis, which he called *Ainulindalë* ("Song of the Holy Ones" in Quenya). That his creation myth should be called a "song" is wholly appropriate to his method, for Tolkien's cosmogony employs the ancient and traditional idea that the universe was called into being with music, and that its continued functioning is in fact musical, with both harmony and discord in its working. The song begins with Eru the Creator urging the Ainur ("Holy Ones") to sing:

> There was Eru, the One, Who in Arda is called Ilúvatar; and he made first the Ainur, the Holy Ones, that were the offspring of his thought, and they were with him before aught else was made. And he spoke to them, propounding to them themes of music; and they sang before him, and he was glad.

Their singing calls forth the universe:

> the music and the echo of the music went out into the Void, and it was not void . . . But when they were come into the Void, Ilúvatar said to them: "Behold your music!" And he showed to them a vision, giving to them sight where before was only hearing; and they saw a new World made visible before them, and it was globed amid the Void, and it was sustained therein (pp. 15, 17).

That cosmogony is musical is a theme in both classical and modern literature. Perhaps its clearest expression in English appears in Dryden's "Song for St. Cecilia's Day, 1687":

From harmony, from heav'nly harmony,
  This universal frame began:
  When Nature underneath a heap
  Of jarring atoms lay,
  And could not heave her head,
  The tuneful voice was heard from high:
  "Arise, ye more than dead."
Then cold and hot and moist and dry
  In order to their stations leap,
  And Music's pow'r obey.
From harmony, from heav'nly harmony
  This universal frame began:
  From harmony to harmony
Thro' all the compass of the notes it ran,
  The diapason closing full in Man.[3]

Dryden drew upon the same classical tradition known to Tolkien, one beginning with Pythagoras' belief in the music of the spheres. As Plato has it in *The Republic*, Book X, each of the heavenly spheres holds a siren, "who goes round with them, hymning a single tone or note."[4] Or as Aristotle, whose clear and scientific mind could not accept this notion, puts it in an attack on Pythagoras, the hard glossy spheres in their rotation rub against each other, causing the sound.[5] More importantly, Tolkien draws upon the classical-Christian tradition that there is an ethical import to the music of the spheres. As the youthful Milton put it in his *Second Prolusion*: "What though no one on earth has ever heard that symphony of the stars? ... let us blame our own impotent ears, which cannot catch the songs or are unworthy to hear such sweet strains ... If our hearts were as pure, as chaste, as snowy as Pythagoras' was, our ears would resound and be filled with that supremely lovely music of the wheeling stars."[6] Cicero observes that the heavenly harmony "is produced by the onward rush of the spheres themselves," and "learned men, by imitating this harmony on stringed instru-

ments and in song, have gained for themselves a return to this
region."[7] Ethical man is in this tradition the capstone, the ultimate act, of creation, as in the final line of Dryden's poem above
and in *Ainulindalë*. For Tolkien, elves and men, the Children of
Ilúvatar, are not part of the music of the Ainur, are not, that
is, merely nature or the physical universe, but rather a special
and unique creation of Eru Himself:

> For the Children of Ilúvatar were conceived by him
> alone; and they came with the third theme, and were not
> in the theme which Ilúvatar propounded in the begin-
> ning, and none of the Ainur had part in their making
> (p. 18).

Tolkien carries on the traditional notion that creation is in
essence musical with the corollary that lack of order in creation
is disharmony, discord:

> as the theme progressed, it came into the heart of Melkor
> to interweave matters of his own imagining that were not
> in accord with the theme of Ilúvatar ... and straightway
> discord arose about him (p. 16).

Christendom too has always seen heaven as a place of musical
harmony, hell and postlapsarian earth places of discord and jarring sound, while the next world, paradise regained, will see a
resolution of all discord and universal harmony restored. We
find the clearest statement of this notion in English poetry in
Milton's "At a Solemn Musick":

> That undisturbed Song of pure concent,
> Ay sung before the saphire-colour'd throne
> To him that sits thereon
> With Saintly shout and solemn Jubily,
> Where the bright Seraphim in burning row
> Their loud-uplifted Angel trumpets blow,
> And the cherubick host in thousand quires
> Touch their immortal Harps of golden wires,
> With those just Spirits that wear victorious Palms,

> Hymns devout and holy psalms
> Singing everlastingly;
> That we on Earth with undiscording voice
> May rightly answer that melodious noise;
> As once we did, till disproportion'd sin
> Jarred against natures chime, and with harsh din
> Broke the fair musick that all creatures made
> To their great Lord, whose love their motion sway'd
> In perfect Diapason, whilst they stood
> In first obedience, and their state of good.
> O may we soon again renew that Song,
> And keep in tune with Heav'n, till God ere long
> To his celestial consort us unite,
> To live with him, and sing in endless morn of light.[8]

Tolkien picks up this theme with his remark that

> never since [the first theme of Ilúvatar] have the Ainur made any music like to this music, though it has been said that a greater still shall be made before Ilúvatar by the choirs of the Ainur and the Children of Ilúvatar after the end of days. Then the themes of Ilúvatar shall be played aright (p. 15).

Tolkien's mythology in *Ainulindalë* thus holds to the Christian pattern of universal history: creation, fall of an angelic being and many of his peers, subsequent universal disharmony for a lengthy period, redemption, end of days, and finally restored universal harmony. We should not be surprised, therefore, to learn that *Ainulindalë*, and indeed all *The Silmarillion*, finds a major source for its themes and structures in the Bible, a work, however, which Tolkien feels free to revise and use for his own creation story. Tolkien expands, explains, and even modifies and puns upon the words of Genesis, thus giving us one of the supreme examples of sub-creative self-confidence: implicitly declaring that one day, perhaps, his mythic cosmogony will supplement, in necessary ways, that of the Bible. This should not be puzzling, in view of what Tolkien says about Scripture in "On Fairy-Stories." If a writer of fantasy, a sub-creator, does his job especially well, Tolkien believes, then his words "may be a far-off gleam or echo of *evangelium* in the real world." Skirting heresy, perhaps, but claiming the highest possible dignity for fantasy, he goes on:

> I would venture to say that approaching the Christian story from this direction, it has long been my feeling (a joyous feeling) that God redeemed the corrupt making-creatures, men, in a way fitting to this aspect, as to others, of their strange nature. The Gospels contain a fairy-story, or a story of a larger kind which embraces all the essence of fairy-stories. They contain many marvels — peculiarly artistic, beautiful and moving: "mythical" in their perfect, self-contained significance.

Tolkien adds to this last sentence a footnote: "The Art is here in the story itself rather than in the telling; for the Author of the story was not the evangelists." [9] The writers both of Scripture and of fairy-stories, works of fantasy, become coworkers with the Great Author, sub-creators working but in accord with the Creator. Tolkien can thus see himself as an ally of the writers of Genesis, and a subaltern of the Author.

He opens *Valaquenta* with an echo of the Bible's first verse: "In the beginning, Eru the One . . . made the Ainur" (p. 25), repeating "In the beginning God created the heaven and the earth." Tolkien likewise echoes, in his own way, the Bible's second verse, as Ilúvatar declares, "I will send forth into the Void the Flame Imperishable" (p. 20). For Tolkien, the "secret fire" and "Imperishable Flame" were symbols or terms for the Holy Spirit.[10] Grasping this, we can hear the echo of Genesis 1:2: "And the earth was without form, and void: . . . And the spirit of God moved . . ." Just as the Creator in Genesis calls his works into existence by Fiat ("Let there be"), so Eru creates with the

same phrase: "Therefore I say *Eä!* Let these things Be!" (p. 20).
Tolkien even has a linguistic pun here: one of the ancient forms
of the Hebrew verb "to be" was *Yah*, the abbreviated third person singular; Tolkien keeps this pronunciation for his version
of the Fiat, changing only the spelling. Moreover, *Ainulindalë*
contains an attempt to solve one of the mysteries of the creation
story in Genesis Chapter One: how it is that light existed before
sun, moon, and stars (Genesis 1:2 describes the first-day creation of light, 1:14–15 the fourth-day creation of the lesser and
greater lights, and the stars). Tolkien has it that when Eru cries
Eä! then suddenly "the Ainur saw afar off a light, as it were a
cloud with a living heart of flame; and they knew that this was
no vision only, but that Ilúvatar had made a new thing: Eä,
the World that Is" (p. 20). Perhaps by espousing the Big Bang
theory, Tolkien urges that light as of flame marks the beginning
of the first nonmental entity — while only later will there come
into being the fruits of the great trees Telperion and Laurelin,
the Sun and Moon (pp. 38–39).

The music accompanying creation in *Ainulindalë* comes
not only from Pythagoras and the classical tradition; Scripture
too depicts the sound of singing as the Almighty works: "When
I laid the foundation of the earth . . . the morning stars sang together, and all the sons of God shouted for joy" (Job 38:4, 7).
Tolkien distantly echoes: "And he spoke to them . . . and they
sang before him, and he was glad" (p. 15). Moreover, Tolkien
presents the Ainur as the subordinate coworkers of Eru in the
acts of creation, in words that echo the Fourth Gospel: "the
Ainur, the Holy Ones, that were the offspring of his thought
. . . were with him before aught else was made" (p. 15); "the
[Word] was in the beginning with God. All things were made
by him; and without him was not anything made" (John 1:2–3).
Some of the Ainur became custodians of Arda, the Earth, which
Tolkien describes in the language of Genesis: "the Earth was
becoming as a garden for their delight" (p. 21); in Scripture,

"the LORD God planted a garden eastward in Eden" (Genesis 2:8): an amateur of Hebrew, Tolkien knew that *eden* means "delight."

Not only were the unfallen Ainur participants in the making of Arda; Melkor was there too, as Satan was in Eden: "in this work the chief part was taken by Manwë and Aulë and Ulmo: but Melkor too was there from the first, and he meddled in all that was done" (p. 20). For just as Scripture describes the fall and subsequent misdeeds of the mighty spirit Satan, who originally stood among the archangels, so Tolkien depicts Melkor:

> To Melkor among the Ainur had been given the greatest gifts of power and knowledge, and he had a share in all the gifts of his brethren. He had often gone alone into the void places seeking the Imperishable Flame (p. 16).

A passage in Ezekiel may lie behind Tolkien's words here:

> Thou hast been in Eden the garden of God ... Thou art the anointed cherub that covereth; and I have set thee so: thou wast upon the holy mountain of God; thou hast walked up and down in the midst of the stones of fire. Thou wast perfect in thy ways from the day that thou wast created, till iniquity was found in thee ... therefore I will cast thee as profane out of the mountain of God (Ezekiel 28:13–16).

The fate of Melkor parallels that of Satan in Revelation:

> From splendour he fell through arrogance to contempt for all things save himself ... he descended through fire and wrath into a great burning, down into Darkness. And darkness he used most in his evil works upon Arda ... But he was not alone. For of the Maiar many were drawn to his splendour in the days of his greatness, and remained in that allegiance down into his darkness (p. 31).

> And the great dragon was cast out, that old serpent, called the Devil, and Satan, which deceiveth the whole world, he was cast out into the earth, and his angels were cast out with him ... Woe unto the inhabiters of the earth and of the sea! for the devil is come down unto you, having great wrath. (Revelation 12:9, 12).

Even the words of Eru after the fall of Melkor, reaffirming his own identity and the need of all to know it, come from a frequently reiterated passage in the Bible:

> Mighty are the Ainur, and mightiest among them is Melkor; but that he may know, and all the Ainur, that I am Ilúvatar ... (p. 17).

> ye shall know that I am the LORD (Exodus 6:7);
> ye shall know that I am the LORD (Ezekiel 14:8).

That Quenya name Ilúvatar, incidentally, is the equivalent in meaning to a standard Hebrew name for God: *ilúvë*, "the all," *tar*, "high" = *El Shaddai*, "God Most High" (Exodus 6:3).

Moving ahead briefly to *Quenta Silmarillion* we find that this work continues both Tolkien's creation myth and his extensive use of the Bible:

> since, when the fires were subdued or buried beneath the primeval hills, there was need of light, Aulë at the prayer of Yavanna wrought two mighty lamps for the lighting of the Middle-earth (p. 35)

just as in Genesis, "God made two great lights" (1:16). Again, in Genesis, after God said "let the earth bring forth grass, and herb yielding seed after its kind, and the tree yielding fruit" (1:11), He created "the living creature after his kind, and cattle after their kind" (1:25). Likewise in Tolkien's work, "there arose a multitude of growing things great and small, mosses and grasses and great ferns, and trees whose tops were crowned with cloud," a work soon followed by the appearance of "beasts" that "came forth and dwelt in the grassy plains" (p. 35). As in the Eden of Genesis there were two trees of power — the trees of life and knowledge — that were to affect forever the fate of men (the eating of one of them brought death to us all, whereas the eating of the other in paradise will someday bring the "healing of nations" — Revelation 22:2) so in Tolkien's paradise Valinor there were "Two Trees... Of all things which Yavanna made they have most renown, and about their fate all the tales of the elder days are woven" (p. 38).

Having felt free to make such extensive use of Genesis, Tolkien felt equally free to modify it for the purposes of his own mythological epic. For whereas Genesis makes clear that man's original destiny was to live forever, a destiny thwarted by his sin and consequent mortality, *Quenta Silmarillion* breaks this thwarted being into two sets of creatures, deathless elves and mortal men: "Elves die not till the world dies, unless they are slain or waste in grief," whereas "the sons of Men die indeed, and leave the world... Death is their fate, the gift of Ilúvatar" (p. 42). Part of the reason for this change comes simply from Tolkien's need to make room for his great tale *Akallabêth*, which uses Genesis in its own way; the rest of the paragraph quoted just above sets the stage for that work: "Death is their fate, the gift of Ilúvatar, which as Time wears even the Powers shall envy. But Melkor has cast his shadow upon it, and confounded it with darkness, and brought forth evil out of good, and fear out of hope." But probably a more important reason for the change is the modern recognition, which could hardly have failed to make its mark on Tolkien, that man, as part of the world of nature, must share in its dying as a necessary corollary to his own living.

At any rate, Tolkien sees man's mortality as a gift and blessing which Melkor has tried to make us see as a curse, whereas in Genesis death is indeed a curse, a punishment laid upon an otherwise deathless being whom Melkor's model and original had beguiled into believing that lack of knowledge of good and evil was a curse rather than a blessed part of an endless and painless existence.

Tolkien had, by the completion of *Ainulindalë* (perhaps in 1918), his quest-object, his questers, his evil antagonist, and a Secondary World for their ambience. His next task was to fill in the gaps between creation, on the one hand, and the redemption made possible by Beren's great deed, on the other. We have seen how he found his inspiration for the first-written later tales in medieval European literature such as *Beowulf*, *The Kalevala*, and *The Mabinogion*, and for his creation story from the Bible; the same combination will hold true for the rest of *The Silmarillion*.

Such a combination of sources, pagan and Christian, should not surprise us, for we find Tolkien supporting its literary validity in his lecture of 1936, *"Beowulf:* The Monsters and the Critics." Attempting to correct what Tolkien regarded as the basic modern misapprehensions of *Beowulf*, the lecture argues that the poem's mythological aspects, especially Grendel and the dragon, are not the aesthetic failures of a childish age, fanciful blemishes upon an otherwise admirable historical poem; rather than an "inexplicable blunder of taste," the monsters are "essential, fundamentally allied to the underlying ideas of the poem, which give it its lofty tone and high seriousness." And those fundamental ideas, he argues, are by direct analogy Christian, having to do with the redemptive power of self-sacrifice (Beowulf dies to save his people) and the conviction that evil and good are most clearly perceived by the imagination in mythological form:

> It is the strength of the northern mythological imagination that it faced this problem [of radical evil], put the

monsters in the centre, gave them victory but no honour, and found a potent but terrible solution in naked will and courage.

Tolkien wished to deny that this mode of "imagination has faded forever into literary ornament," and to reassert that it has "power, as it were, to revive its spirit even in our own times." [11] It already had in *The Silmarillion* and *The Hobbit.*

Not only is the mythology vital to the poem, so is the Christianity, Tolkien argues in opposition to what he regards as the second modern misapprehension of *Beowulf*: that its Anglo-Saxon creators "could not . . . keep Scandinavian bogies and the Scriptures separate in their puzzled brains," [12] that the poem is a confused and flawed mixture of pagan and Christian notions. He urges that such blending of mythologies strengthens rather than weakens the work, that its author, standing as he did in a moment of historical shift, pagan to Christian, already himself on the Christian side but still alive to the ancient traditions, was able to view his tales from a special perspective: since he "could view from without, but still feel immediately and from within, the old dogma," we have in *Beowulf*

> a poem from a pregnant moment of poise, looking back into the pit [of paganism], by a man learned in old tales who was struggling, as it were, to get a general view of them all, perceiving their common tragedy of inevitable ruin, and yet feeling this more poetically because he was himself removed from the direct pressure of its despair.[13]

Ancient, pre-Christian tales seen through the eyes of a Christian writer — as apt a description of *The Silmarillion* as of *Beowulf*; indeed, this is the way Tolkien himself saw his work, according to its editor, Christopher Tolkien:

> my father came to conceive *The Silmarillion* as a compilation, a compendious narrative, made long afterwards from sources of great diversity (poems, and annals, and

oral tales) that had survived in agelong tradition (*Silmarillion*, p. 8).

It is no accident that this description of *The Silmarillion* is an equally apt description of the Bible. Like Scripture, *The Silmarillion* is about creation, fall, redemption, and apocalypse. Since these are the largest and most nearly ultimate subjects the human mind can frame concerning its own fate, it can only deal with them, Tolkien believes — as did Milton — mythologically. As Milton's Raphael says to Adam:

> how shall I relate
> To human sense th'invisible exploits
> Of warring Spirits?

Raphael's method is Milton's justification for writing mythological poetry:

> what surmounts the reach
> Of human sense, I shall delineate so,
> By lik'ning spiritual to corporeal forms.

Milton, like Tolkien after him, is well aware that mythology presents suprahuman ideas told in human terms, "as if it were so." Yet both writers pull back from the logical implication of their literary understanding of myth, that "it isn't really so," with an intellectual sleight of hand. As Raphael suggests:

> though what if Earth
> Be but the shadow of Heav'n, and things therein
> Each to other like, more than on Earth is thought?
>   (V, 574–6).

What if the human terms of myths really do correspond to spiritual reality? This is precisely Tolkien's way of dealing with the objection that a myth is only a cipher dressed-up with a lie. When he was in the process of converting C. S. Lewis to Christianity, Tolkien had to answer Lewis's unbeliever's argument

that "myths are lies, even though lies breathed through silver."
Tolkien responded, as his poem "Mythopoeia" (quoted at the
beginning of this chapter) shows, that mythmaking is simply
man's way of acting like God, of being sub-creative and therefore most fully himself, and to this extent mythmaking truly
reflects reality. "We make by the law in which we're made . . .
and not only made, but made in the image and likeness of a
Maker." The light dawning (he too had carefully pondered
Milton), Lewis asks, as Carpenter recreates the conversation:

> you mean . . . that the story of Christ is simply a true
> myth, a myth that works on us in the same way as the
> others, but a myth that *really happened?* In that case, he
> said, I begin to understand (Carpenter, p. 148).

I suppose that Tolkien nodded something like Yes, the Evangelists wrote a true myth; and in so doing, he may have thought
even then of the Epilogue he was soon to write for "On Fairy-
Stories," in which he asserts the corollary of the same notion:
that a successful fantasy "may be a far-off gleam or echo of
evangelium in the real world." This is the very issue I raise
concerning *The Silmarillion*, a work already finished in its es-
sentials when Tolkien wrote that

> Probably every writer making a secondary world, a fan-
> tasy, every sub-creator, wishes in some measure to be a
> real maker, or hopes he is drawing on reality: hopes that
> the peculiar quality of this secondary world (if not the
> details) are derived from Reality, or are flowing into it.

There may be, he suggests, an even deeper reality underlying
successful fantasy, the same reality that for Tolkien is "true" in
Christian myth:

> I would venture to say . . . approaching the Christian
> Story from this direction . . . that God redeemed the cor-
> rupt making-creatures, men, in a way fitting to this as-

pect . . . The Gospels contain a fairy-story, or a story of
a larger kind which embraces all the essence of fairy-
stories . . . [and are] "mythical" in their perfect, self-
contained significance.[14]

In the Gospels, which deal mythically with the story of redemption, "the desire and aspiration of sub-creation has been
raised to the fulfillment of Creation." Being thus a "true myth"
the fairy-story of the "Evangelium has not abrogated legends;
it has hallowed them." A successful fantasy, therefore, by dealing in its own terms with the themes of the Gospels and the
rest of the Bible, could bring to the reader "exactly the same
quality, if not the same degree" of the Christian "joy" Tolkien
says is the gift of fairy-story. If this is so, then the author of
fairy-story does well to feel that "in Fantasy he may actually
assist in" the divine work, "the effoliation and multiple enrich-
ment of creation." [15]

Here stands Tolkien's justification for the audacity he
shows in *Ainulindalë* — rewriting and supplementing Scripture.
And the rest of *The Silmarillion* does the same; it tells a mythological story of creation, fall, redemption, and apocalypse in its
own terms, setting up a cosmos, a secondary world parallel to
our own, letting us see that world go through the same process
of fall that enmeshes us, and then granting us the privilege of a
glimpse ahead at our own world's redemption, seen analogically,
as a lost Silmaril is regained and returned to Valinor, and Morgoth (Tolkien's Satan) is destroyed.

The extensive use and revision of Scripture continues.
Tolkien's biblically parallel myth of the fall of Satan comes
early in *Quenta Silmarillion*. When Melkor summons ambition
and evil into his own heart — after the manner of his original,
Satan — he must be expelled from Arda, as Satan is expelled
from heaven. To aid the Valar in this effort comes a mighty
equivalent of an archangel, Tulkas:

hearing in the far heaven that there was battle in the
Little Kingdom . . . came Tulkas the Strong, whose anger
passes like a mighty wind, scattering cloud and darkness
before it; and Melkor fled before his wrath and his
laughter, and forsook Arda, and there was peace for a
long age. And Tulkas remained and became one of the
Valar of the Kingdom of Arda; but Melkor brooded in
the outer darkness, and his hate was given to Tulkas for
ever after (p. 35).

The ultimate source of this passage is Revelation, though Tolkien gets his idea by way of an intermediary, Milton. The last
book in the Bible tells us that

there was war in heaven: Michael and his angels fought
against the dragon; the dragon fought and his angels,
          And prevailed not; neither was their place found
any more in heaven.
          And the great dragon was cast out, that old ser-
pent, called the Devil.

The result of the battle and ouster is "Woe to the inhabiters of
the earth and of the sea! for the devil is come down unto you,
having great wrath, because he knoweth that he hath but a
short time" (Revelation 12:7–9, 12). Note that Revelation dates
the expulsion of Satan quite near the End, the Apocalypse ("he
hath but a short time"), whereas Tolkien dates his version of
this event near the beginning of creation, even before man appears. The reason is quite simple: Milton does the same. His
mythological epic, *Paradise Lost*, depicts Satan's expulsion from
heaven with language and events clearly influential over Tolkien. In Book VI of his work, Milton depicts a great and lengthy
battle between Satan and his forces, and the angels of God. Two
full days of heavenly warfare end with a virtual draw and a
badly damaged cosmos: the "seated hills" have been "plukt"
from their places, the "bottom of the Mountains upward turn'd"

and flung upon the still unvanquished demonic host. Viewing the destruction, God sends his Son to finish the battle, "since none but thou/ Can end it" (VI, 643, 649, 702–3). Likewise in *The Silmarillion*, Tulkas comes from "far heaven" to end the till-now indecisive battle that is heavily damaging the cosmos. At his approach "Melkor fled before his wrath," as at the ap- proach of the Son, Satan and his angels "headlong themselves they threw/ Down from the verge of Heaven, Eternal wrath" burning after them (VI, 864–5).

Just as Tolkien's version of the creation and the fall and expulsion of his version of Satan is biblically based, so is his mythological version of redemption, a theme that begins to find clear statement near the end of *Quenta Silmarillion*. After the destruction of Turgon and his realm, "Morgoth thought that his triumph was fulfilled." And so it seemed, but for the continued concern of the Valar for the Two Kindreds; for

> it is said that in that time Ulmo came to Valinor out of the deep waters, and spoke there to the Valar of the need of the Elves; and he called on them to forgive them, and rescue them from the overmastering might of Morgoth, and win back the Silmarils ... But Manwë moved not; and of the counsels of his heart what tale shall tell? The wise have said that the hour was not yet come, and that only one speaking in person for the cause of both Elves and men, pleading for pardon on their misdeeds and pity on their woes, might move the counsels of the Powers (p. 244).

Only one who, as it were, shared in the nature and destiny of both men and elves, and who might speak for them both, could move the forgiveness of the Powers. Who might this be? *Eala Earendel!* Now Tolkien sees how his years-old vision of the apotheosis of Eärendil, his exaltation to the heavens like Christ's, could be made to fit the shape his mythological epic was taking. Who, after all, is this Earendel of Anglo-Saxon poetry, what

does he signify? According to Cynewulf's poem, he is in fact
a symbol of Christ, as the lines succeeding the passage *"Eala
Earendel engla beorhtast . . ."* that was so important to Tolkien's
imagination show:

> Lo! thou Splendor of the dayspring, fairest of angels sent
> to men upon earth, thou Radiance of the Sun of Right-
> eousness, bright beyond the stars, Thou of Thy very self
> dost illumine all the tides of time! Even as Thou, God
> begotten of God, Son of the true Father, didst ever dwell
> without beginning in the glory of heaven, so Thine own
> handiwork in its present need imploreth Thee with con-
> fidence that Thou send us the bright sun, and come in
> Thy very person to enlighten those who have long been
> covered with murky cloud, and sitting here in dark-
> ness.[16]

Tolkien knew from the beginning that his Eärendil was
a poetic representative or type of Christ, and so he appears in
The Silmarillion: "Bright Eärendil" desires deeply "to find perhaps the last shore, and bring ere he died the message of Elves
and Men to the Valar in the West, that should move their hearts
to pity for the sorrows of Middle-earth" (p. 246). Later, Ulmo
declares that "For this he was born into the world" (p. 249),
echoing, in advance, Christ's words to Pilate: "To this end was
I born, and for this cause came I into the world" (John 18:37).
Again, as Jesus is held by Christians to be the son of a human
woman and the divine Spirit, so Tolkien presents Eärendil as
one of mixed ancestry, half-human half-elven. As Ulmo asks
Mandos, "say unto me, whether is he Eärendil Tuor's son of the
line of Hador, or the son of Idril, Turgon's daughter, of the
Elven-house of Finwë?" (p. 249). Willingness to sacrifice self
is of the essence of a type of Christ. As Eärendil, disembarking
upon the shore of Valinor, says to his wife, "Here none but myself shall set foot, lest you fall under the wrath of the Valar.
But that peril I will take on myself alone, for the sake of the

Two Kindreds" (p. 248), a speech reminiscent of Paul's words about Christ:

> Christ redeemed us from the curse of the law, being made a curse for us (Galatians 3:13).

After his long and difficult journey to Valinor — Tolkien's version of heaven — Eärendil presents himself, bearer of the Silmaril, to Manwë, offering his plea for the Two Kindreds. When he appears, Eönwë, herald of Manwë, declares Tolkien's altered version of Cynewulf's *Eala Earendel*, again in words clearly descriptive of an adumbration of Christ:

> Hail Eärendil, of mariners most renowned, the looked for that cometh at unawares, the longed for that cometh beyond hope! Hail Eärendil, bearer of light before the Sun and Moon! Splendour of the Children of Earth, star in the darkness, jewel in the sunset, radiant in the morning!

Like the Earendel of Cynewulf's poem, Tolkien's Eärendil appears prophetically as the evening and morning star he will become — both of them figures of the Christ of the New Testament. Eärendil's appearance before the court of Manwë bearing the Silmaril, having willingly risked the curse of the Valar, to present his plea for the forgiveness of the Two Kindreds seems strongly reminiscent of the risen Christ's appearance, recounted in symbolic language in *Hebrews*, before the heavenly throne to present the gift of his sacrifice and to plead for men's forgiveness:

> Eärendil went into Valinor and to the halls of Valimar, and never again set foot upon the lands of Men . . . And Eärendil stood before their faces, and delivered the errand of the Two Kindreds. Pardon he asked for the Noldor and pity for their great sorrows, and mercy upon Men and Elves and succour in their need. And his prayer was granted (p. 249).

According to the *Letter to the Hebrews,* Christ "by his own blood . . . entered at once into the holy place, having obtained eternal redemption for us." He entered, that is, "into heaven itself, now to appear in the presence of God for us . . . Now once in the end of the world hath he appeared to put away sin by the sacrifice of himself" (Hebrews 9:12, 24, 26). The result, in both mythologies, is the same. All the power of the West attacked Morgoth, and "his feet were hewn from under him, and he was hurled upon his face. Then he was bound with the chain Angainor which he had worn aforetime . . . Morgoth himself the Valar thrust through the door of Night beyond the Vales of the World, into the Timeless Void, and a guard is set for ever on those walls" (pp. 252–5). For this mythological event Tolkien has blended passages in First Samuel and Revelation. In the former, the God Dagon was found "fallen upon his face to the earth before the Ark of the Lord" (I Samuel 5:3). In the Bible's last book, Tolkien found described the imprisonment of Satan, who is bound with "a great chain," and "cast . . . into the bottomless pit," with a "seal" set upon him (Revelation 20:1–3). With this, the outline of Tolkien's own version of Apocalypse is complete.

III

Reading
Quenta Silmarillion

ଏ

WITH THE CREATION of his Secondary World, here called Arda, the realm of Manwë, Tolkien has set the stage for his longest narrative, the Tale of the Silmarilli, their creation, loss, recapture, and doom. If this sequence seems familiar, that is because it repeats with regard to particular objects the overall pattern of the larger work itself — creation, fall, redemption, and apocalypse. The pattern is of course biblical and Miltonic in origin, though there is an obvious difference, as we might expect, given Tolkien's Christian understanding of Scripture: the Bible's pattern is unique and once-for-all, whereas Tolkien's stands as a type to the Bible's antitype, a smaller prefigurative version, and its pattern is often repeated: *Quenta Silmarillion*'s version of the fall and dispersal of elves recurs, with regard to men, in *Akallabêth*, and there are smaller, local repetitions. In contrast to the Bible's ultimate myth, there stands Tolkien's version, a myth of the eternal return of evil, one stated most clearly in *The Fellowship of the Ring*: "Always after a defeat and a respite, the Shadow takes another shape and grows again" (I, 60).

Though Tolkien's overall themes are biblical, the story of the Silmarils found its inspiration in the same work he mined for his tale of Túrin Turambar — *The Kalevala* — and in particular its story of the creation and theft of the Sampo. In Runes 10, 42–43, and 47–49 of *The Kalevala* Tolkien found the source of much of the outline of the Silmarils' story. In that work the blacksmith hero Ilmarinen forges his great treasure, the Sampo, a work much coveted by his antagonist, the wicked Louhi, even as Fëanor has made the Silmarilli, objects much coveted by Tolkien's antagonist Melkor. Tolkien has, however, divided some of his source's characters in two; his counterpart to Ilmarinen is both Fëanor who made the Silmarils and Beren who must recapture one of them. Ilmarinen wishes to wed the daughter of Louhi, and to gain the privilege of wooing her he must give the Sampo to Louhi, as Beren, wishing to marry Lúthien, the daughter of Thingol, must bring him a Silmaril in exchange for her hand. Louhi is in this sense thus the original of both Thingol and Melkor. Ilmarinen provides the Sampo, but fails to win the love of Louhi's daughter. In revenge he steals back the Sampo with the help of his kinsman Wainamoinen. Thus Ilmarinen too becomes a partial source for the action of Melkor, his theft of the Silmarils. Tolkien seems also to have borrowed the housing of the Silmarils from *The Kalevala*: Louhi has hidden the Sampo in "the copper-bearing mountains" "behind nine locks of copper,/ In the stone-berg of Pohyola."[1] Fëanor has hidden his treasure "in a strong place and treasury in the hills; and there in Formenos ... the Silmarils were shut in a chamber of iron" (p. 71).

In her frenzied efforts to regain the Sampo Louhi only manages to destroy it, sending its pieces floating in the ocean, even as the violent efforts of the sons of Fëanor to regain the Silmarils result in the sinking of one of them in the sea, another's loss in the earth. The third Silmaril, of course, comes to Eärendil, who bears it in his ship to travel across the heavens as a new star, a tale partly originating in Tolkien's knowledge of the ending of *The Kalevala*, in which Wainamoinen sails in *his* ship to heaven; he

Sang himself a boat of copper,
Beautiful his boat of magic . . .
Singing as he left Wainola,
This his plaintive song and echo:
"Suns may rise and set in Suomi,
Rise and set for generations . . .
Then will Suomi need my coming,
Watch for me at dawn of morning,
That I may bring back the Sampo,
Bring anew the harp of joyance,
Bring again the golden moonlight,
Bring again the silver sunshine,
Peace and plenty to the Northland."
In his copper-bonded vessel
Left his tribe in Kalevala . . .
Sailing to the fiery sunset,
To the higher-landed regions,
To the lower verge of heaven.[2]

Later, in her hatred of Ilmarinen and Wainamoinen, Louhi comes to their land of Kalevala to steal the sun and moon, bringing darkness, woe, and sterility, as Melkor's theft of the Silmarils and destruction of the Two Trees does the same to Valinor:

Louhi, hostess of Pohyola,
Northland's old and toothless wizard,
Makes the sun and moon her captives;
In her arms she takes fair Luna
From her cradle in the birch tree,
Calls the Sun down from his station,
From the fir-tree's bending branches,
Carries them to upper Northland,
To the darksome Sariola.[3]

Melkor, too, we remember, carried the Silmarils to the uttermost north of Arda. In Tolkien's work the Two Trees, Tel-

perion and Laurelin, manage to sprout before their death a last
flower and fruit, the moon and sun — an expansion of the story
in *The Kalevala,* in which Ilmarinen attempts to create new
lights to replace the stolen ones, but fails. Louhi's theft included
not only sun and moon, but fire also, and Wainamoinen's recapture of what the work calls the "fire-child" provided some
of the background of the story of the regaining of a Silmaril by
Beren and Lúthien. In the Finnish epic, the fire-child ends up in
the bellies of a number of progressively larger fish, greatly
distressing the creatures, even as the Silmaril ends up in the belly
of Carcharoth, who is greatly pained by its presence. As Carcharoth must be killed and slit open for the Silmaril to be rescued, so must the fish:

> Quick a knife falls from the heavens,
> From the clouds a magic fish-knife,
> Silver edged and golden-headed
> To the girdle of the sun-child;
> Quick he grasps the copper handle,
> Quick the hero carves the fire-pike,
> Finds therein the tortured lake-trout;
> Carves the lake-trout thus discovered,
> Finds therein the fated whiting . . .
> Finds the ball of fire within it.[4]

Thus in many of its details the story of the Silmarils is a recasting of the story of Ilmarinen, Wainamoinen, and the Sampo.
But again, as in his use of the Kullervo story in the "Tale of
Túrin Turambar," Tolkien has deepened and enriched what
he has taken from *The Kalevala,* by attaching it to a major
theme, the history of a world and its fate, and by giving it a
more powerful mythological cast; he has, that is, attached his
version of the Sampo tale to a revision of the Bible, and struc-
tured it according to a strong and resonant pattern — the overarching laws of his Secondary World. Those laws affect the

success of a large and complex narrative pattern, a tale in which the creation of the Silmarils is on the one hand an act "snared" in the web of Melkor and on the other hand part of the overall plan of Ilúvatar that will result in the annihilation of Morgoth, the peopling of Middle-earth with mankind, and the eventual homecoming of all elves to the realm of the Valar. That this should be so is related to Tolkien's insistence in his essay "On Fairy-Stories" that each Secondary World must work according to its own imaginative principles or laws, not those of the Primary World. For if the "real" world and its expectations intrude, the enchanted imagination falters:

> What really happens is that the story-maker proves a successful "sub-creator." He makes a Secondary World which your mind can enter. Inside it, what he relates is "true": it accords with the laws of that world. You therefore believe it, while you are, as it were, inside. The moment disbelief arises, the spell is broken; the magic, or rather art, has failed. You are then out in the primary world again, looking at the little abortive Secondary World from outside.[5]

Thus, to discover the narrative principles underlying the story of a Secondary World one needs to get at the peculiar "laws" of the world itself; for those laws find narrative expression in the themes of a work of fantasy. To put it another way, the deepest moral wishes and sacred dreams of a successful sub-creator, even those unknown to him consciously, form the ethics and metaphysics of his story. As Tolkien once wrote to Father Robert Murray, who had commended his work as a book "entirely about grace":

> *The Lord of the Rings* is of course a fundamentally religious and Catholic work; unconsciously so at first but consciously in the revision ... For the religious element is absorbed into the story and the symbolism.[6]

We may say something very similar about *The Silmarillion*. Its
central structuring principle is the Judaeo-Christian belief in an
omnipotent divine Being with a conscious plan for history, Who
intends, even within the apparent victories of evil and darkness,
an ultimate goodness. This idea finds multiple expressions in *The
Silmarillion*, the first of them Ilúvatar's prediction to Melkor that

> thou ... shalt see that no theme may be played that hath
> not its uttermost source in me, nor can any alter the
> music in my despite. For he that attempteth this shall
> prove but mine instrument in the devising of things more
> wonderful, which he himself hath not imagined (p. 17).

Manwë later echoes these words:

> Thus even as Eru spoke to us shall beauty not before
> conceived be brought into Eä, and evil yet be good to
> have been (p. 98).

Ilúvatar again states the same principle differently:

> thou, Melkor, wilt discover all the secret thoughts of
> thy mind, and wilt perceive that they are but part of
> the whole and tributary to its glory (p. 17).

What Tolkien throughout *The Silmarillion* calls "fate" or
"doom" really means the hidden will of Ilúvatar, controlling for
good the destinies of all Arda and its overlords and inhabitants.
Yet fate is not merely applied from outside a character; it is
paradoxically the expression of his own free nature as that
nature exists within Eru; for each character in *The Silmarillion*,
whether evil or good, stands before Ilúvatar with both free will
and the certainty that whatever he wills shall turn out, like the
acts of Melkor, as but a "part of the whole and tributary to its
glory." This too is of course a traditional Christian theme, perhaps best stated in *Paradise Lost*, where Milton says of Satan
that his fate will always be such that he

> enrag'd might see
> How all his malice serv'd but to bring forth
> Infinite goodness (I, 216–218).

Or, as Mephistopheles says to Faust, he is a

> part of that Power
> Which always wills evil, always procures good.[7]

Like the beings of Arda, Milton's characters find themselves and all their acts paradoxically both free and foreknown:

> As if Predestination over-rul'd
> Thir will, dispos'd by absolute Decree
> Or high foreknowledge; they themselves decreed
> Thir own revolt, not I: if I foreknew,
> Foreknowledge had no influence on thir fault,
> Which had no less prov'd certain unforeknown
> (III, 114–119).

Milton sees any attempt to clarify the paradox as only the work of devils; for in hell appears this constant debate:

> Of Providence, Foreknowledge, Will, and Fate,
> Fixt Fate, Free Will, Foreknowledge absolute,
> And found no end, in wand'ring mazes lost (II, 558–561).

The logical difficulties of the fate–free-will controversy trap Tolkien just as they trap Milton's devils. Though Ilúvatar determined that men "should have a virtue to shape their life, amid the powers and chances of the world, beyond the music of the Ainur, which is as fate to all things else" (p. 41), Tolkien yet insists, for example, that Beren has a "great doom upon him" (p. 165), is "defended by fate," and has ideas "put into his heart" (p. 164). This is, I suppose, one of the reasons why Christopher Tolkien warns that a "complete consistency . . . is not to be looked for" in *The Silmarillion* (p. 8). Still we may presume that Tolkien wishes his characters to be at least as free as Milton's either to fall or be great.

Corollary to the theme of fate is what might be called the Second Law of Arda: the power of the oath, curse, or prophecy. In Tolkien's Secondary World, such things have a real existence and power, and work to structure the action throughout *Quenta Silmarillion*. They can be imposed from without, as a consequence of an evil action (the Doom of Mandos), or from within, as an initiator of an evil action (the Oath of Fëanor); the latter lies behind a great many of the evil deeds in the story:

> They swore an oath which none shall break, and none should take, by the name even of Ilúvatar, calling the Everlasting Dark upon them if they kept it not... vowing to pursue with vengeance and hatred to the ends of the World Vala, Demon, Elf or Man as yet unborn, or any creature, great or small, good or evil, that time should bring forth unto the end of days, whoso should hold or take or keep a Silmaril from their possession (p. 83).

Thence comes the evil worked in *The Silmarillion* by the sons of Fëanor. The spell of doom imposed from without, called the "Prophecy of the North, and the Doom of the Noldor," was spoken by Mandos himself, and structures all else in the tale that relates to the search for the Silmarils; it confirmed and made clear the evil effects of the Oath of Fëanor:

> Tears unnumbered ye shall shed; and the Valar will fence Valinor against you, and shut you out, so that not even the echo of your lamentation shall pass over the mountains. On the House of Fëanor the wrath of the Valar lieth from the West unto the uttermost East, and upon all that will follow them it shall be laid also. Their Oath shall drive them, and yet betray them, and ever snatch away the very treasures that they have sworn to pursue. To evil end shall all things turn that they begin well; and by treason of kin unto kin, and the fear of treason, shall this come to pass (p. 88).

Mention of the Silmarils brings us to the Third Law of Arda, which I call the Law of Creativity. The urge to make and build, for good or ill, fills the inhabitants of Tolkien's Secondary World; for many in Arda would say with their creator that "we make still by the law in which we're made," that we make "because we are made... in the image and likeness of a Maker." A typical expression of this law, and one echoed in "On Fairy-Stories," appears in Aulë's untimely creation of the dwarves:

> so greatly did Aulë desire the coming of the Children, to have learners to whom he could teach his lore and his crafts, that he was unwilling to await the fulfilment of the designs of Ilúvatar. And Aulë made the Dwarves.

When challenged by Eru ("Why hast thou done this?") Aulë answers:

> I desired things other than I am, to love and to teach them... And in my impatience I have fallen into folly. Yet the making of things is in my heart from my own making by thee (p. 43).

Though misshapen and untimely, the dwarves become necessary actors in the story of the Silmarils; the Third Law thus appears as an outgrowth (as they are all) of the First.

Of course the major expression of this law, and the formative event of the tale, is the fashioning of the Silmarils, for Aulë passes his creative urge and power on to the Noldor: from Aulë, says Tolkien,

> comes the lore and knowledge of the Earth... the lore of all craftsmen: the weaver, the shaper of wood, and the worker in metals... Aulë it is who is named the Friend of the Noldor, for of him they learned much in after days... The Noldor also it was who first achieved the making of gems; and the fairest of all gems were the Silmarils (p. 39).

The urge to create began as a good gift, and the receiver in greatest measure of that gift was Fëanor: "he it was who, first of the Noldor, discovered how gems greater and brighter than those of the Earth might be made with skill" (p. 64). As his mastery grew, Fëanor pondered his greatest creation, and though he was "driven by the fire of his own heart only," he nonetheless was "snared . . . in the webs of Melkor's malice against the Valar" (p. 66), so that when he made those "three great jewels" from the "blended light of the Trees of Valinor," he had created such objects of desire that as "Mandos foretold . . . the fates of Arda, earth, sea, and air, lay locked within them" (p. 67). Tolkien has thus arranged the events of his narrative in such a way that the creation of the Silmarils is in the short view a working out of the evil will of Melkor and in the ultimate view part of the overall plan of Eru that will result in the annihilation of Morgoth, the peopling of Middle-earth with humankind, and the eventual homecoming of all elves to the realm of the Valar.

The last of the structuring laws of Arda I call the Enchantment of Beauty. This law has two faces, the two responses to beauty: love and lust. The first desires love in response from the beloved, the second only covets possession of an object, whether animate or inanimate. The one is good in Middle-earth, the other evil, but both work toward the fulfillment of Eru's master plan.

Fëanor's creativity brings about the first occasion for the working of this law's second phase. After the creation of the Silmarils, all who dwell in Aman are "filled with wonder and delight" at their beauty, but one of them responds with yet another mood: "Melkor lusted for the Silmarils," and "sought ever more eagerly how he should destroy Fëanor and end the friendship of the Valar and the Elves" (p. 67). From this lust and hatred will come eventually the annihilation of Melkor, but not until several positive applications of the law come to pass.

Indeed the existence of one of those partly responsible for
Melkor's end becomes possible as a result of that law, and even
before the Silmarils are made — Lúthien, born of Elwë's enchantment by Melian. Moving westward with his people in
response to the summons of the Valar, Elwë chances upon
Melian near the River Gelion: "there suddenly he heard the song
of nightingales. Then an enchantment fell on him, and he stood
still . . . he heard the voice of Melian . . . . and being filled with
love Elwë came to her and took her hand." Of their union was
born Lúthien, "the fairest of all the children of Ilúvatar that was
or shall ever be" (pp. 55–6).

But that is to be in the future. Meanwhile, the Silmarils
exert their enchantment even on their maker: "Fëanor began to
love the Silmarils with a greedy love, and grudged the sight of
them to all save to his father and his seven sons" (p. 69).

The object and the occasion now exist for Melkor's
vengeance, a way to come between the elves and Valar with
the Silmarils and the power they represent. Once again Tolkien
models his account of a fall on the biblical story in Genesis.
Quietly and subtly, Melkor spreads lies, saying that the Powers
of Aman had brought elves to their realm not for their good
but out of jealousy, "fearing that the beauty of the Quendi and
the makers' power that Ilúvatar had bequeathed to them would
grow too great for the Valar to govern" (p. 68). Just such a
lie did the serpent speak in Eden, suggesting to Eve that the
Prohibition came not for man's good but out of the jealous fear
that, eating, "ye shall be as gods, knowing good and evil" (Genesis 3:5). In a creature of imagination, already endowed with
creative desire, such a lie is like a flame; as Tolkien says of
Melkor's work, "he that sows lies in the end shall not lack of a
harvest" (p. 68). Melkor's next lie concerned the new creatures
soon to come: "now the whisper went among the Elves that
Manwë held them captive, so that Men might come and supplant
them in the kingdoms of Middle-earth" (p. 68). Thus the two

plans of Melkor became in fact one: "Fiercest burned the new flame of desire for freedom and wider realms in the eager heart of Fëanor; and Melkor laughed in his secrecy, for to that mark his lies had been addressed, hating Fëanor above all, and lusting ever for the Silmarils" (p. 68).

In the short term, Melkor's plan works in his favor. Fëanor begins "openly to speak words of rebellion against the Valar, crying aloud that he would depart from Valinor" (p. 69), causing for the first time unrest in that land, the wearing of arms and speaking of angry words. For having threatened his half-brother Fingolfin with a sword (a weapon introduced by Melkor) Fëanor is banished from Tirion for twelve years, another event furthering the plan of Melkor; for Fëanor's fortress at Formenos, far to the north, will be hidden from the Valar and more open to Melkor's attack. With the next festival of harvest comes the fruition of evil; accompanied by the great spider Ungoliant, Melkor, soon to be called Morgoth the Black Enemy, re-enters Aman and, with Fëanor at the feast among the Valar, attacks Formenos and steals the Silmarils, killing Finwë. Melkor wreaks double vengeance, not only taking the father and the treasure from Fëanor whom he hates, but destroying the Two Trees of the Valar, whom he hates even more. But with the destruction of the lights of Aman, Tolkien introduces another version of his central theme: that though there is an evil, a darkness no power of good can pierce or destroy, yet it will in the end destroy itself:

> In that hour was made a Darkness that seemed not a lack but a thing with being of its own: for it was indeed made by malice out of Light (p. 76).

Not even the eye of Manwë can pierce that darkness. And yet the dark is made of light; it contains the seed of its own destruction. Tolkien has implicitly paralleled this scene with one in

Ainulindalë in which Melkor's malice only brings about more beauty. As Ilúvatar says to Ulmo:

> Melkor hath made war upon thy province. He hath bethought him of bitter cold immoderate, and yet hath not destroyed the beauty of thy fountains, nor of thy clear pools. Behold the snow, and the cunning work of frost! Melkor hath devised heats and fire without restraint... Behold rather the height and glory of the clouds, and the everchanging mists; and listen to the fall of rain upon the Earth! (p. 19).

As Manwë says, "evil [shall] yet be good to have been" (p. 98), and though Melkor achieve his vengeance, the very objects of his greed will bring about his doom; indeed Lúthien's parents, and Eärendil's great-grandparents, stand already on the scene.

Tolkien finds yet another way to present this notion implicitly. The light that is the enemy of Melkor, the symbol of his ultimate downfall, is the very thing he bears away from Aman triumphantly clutched in his hand: "The Light of the Trees has passed away," says Yavanna, "and lives now only in the Silmarils of Fëanor. Foresighted was he!" (p. 78). In a way that none perceives, Yavanna will prove to be right.

Morgoth's evil fathers more, but again in a way assuring his downfall. He creates toward himself the eternal vigilant hatred of Fëanor and his sons, and brings about the valiant, if destructive, flight of the Noldor from Valinor to Middle-earth and a five-hundred-years' war of vengeance against Thangorodrim: "After Morgoth to the ends of the Earth! War shall he have and hatred undying," shouts Fëanor, and his powerful voice persuades the greater part of the elves. Had they not gone, Tuor could not have met Idril, nor could Eärendil have been born; Beren could not have received the necessary help of Finrod, or Lúthien the help of Huan, and Middle-earth would yet be unpeopled with those moved by elvish enchantment.

In his hatred, Fëanor inspires his sons with his terrible oath, a prime mover in the story of the Silmarils. The efforts of the seven sons to keep that oath lie behind the machinations of much of the latter part of *Quenta Silmarillion*, while the flight of the Noldor, inspired by Fëanor's lust for vengeance against the killer of his father and the thief of the Silmarils, will result in the events of the middle parts of the work, the establishment and history of the kingdoms of the elves: Turgon in Gondolin and Finrod in Nargothrond. Thingol's kingdom in Doriath comes, of course, not from the flight but from his marriage to Melian the Maia; however, he too finds himself drawn into the Doom of Mandos because of his demand of a Silmaril for Lúthien's hand.

In order to grasp the structure of the middle parts of *Quenta Silmarillion* we need to examine the elvish genealogies. Miriel, the first wife of Finwë, died producing her greatest work, Fëanor, leaving her husband in grief. Years later, he found comfort in the love of Indis the Fair, falling under the enchantment of her beauty and fathering on her Finarfin and Fingolfin. Though their love was honorable, the "wedding of his father was not pleasing to Fëanor":

> many saw the effect of this breach within the house of Finwë, judging that if Finwë had endured his loss and been content with the fathering of his mighty son, the courses of Fëanor would have been otherwise, and great evil might have been prevented... But the children of Indis were great and glorious, and their children also; and if they had not lived the history of the Eldar would have been diminished (p. 65).

Indeed the events of *Quenta Silmarillion* and the destruction of Morgoth would not have happened but for Finwë's love of Indis, for she bears Finarfin, father of Finrod, without whom Beren's quest might have failed, and Fingolfin, father of Turgon

and the Silmarils

ll swear, and
hall any-
130).
rin;

who brought about the end of
the "great evils" of Fëanor, the
ctly affects Elwë Thingol, brother
when he hears of the Kinslaying,
h to the sons of Fëanor, divorcing
eriand until the coming of Beren,
ithien) that might otherwise not
have happened.

Thus the half-brothers, the sons of Finwë, Fëanor of Miriel and Finarfin and Fingolfin of Indis, become the progenitors of the action in *Quenta Silmarillion*. The middle parts of the work recount the doings of those lines: Turgon son of Fingolfin founds Gondolin, out of which will come Eärendil, Finrod son of Finarfin founds Nargothrond, a center of concern for both Túrin and Beren.

The events of the middle parts of the work stand under a doom, the "curse and prophecy" of Mandos, who declares to Fëanor and "all that will follow" him: "To evil end shall all things turn that they begin well; and by treason of kin unto kin, and the fear of treason, shall this come to pass" (p. 88). Even the flight fulfills this prophecy. After seizing the ships of the Teleri, Fëanor and his host sail to Endor and then burn the vessels, leaving Fingolfin and his elves stranded; seeing the flames to the east, "they knew that they were betrayed. This was the firstfruits of the Kinslaying and the Doom of the Noldor" (p. 90). After this Fingolfin, Finrod, Turgon, and the others never again trust Fëanor or his sons; the fear of treason poisons all their intercourse.

The first great fortress-kingdom of the Noldor in Beleriand to rise, and the first to fall, Nargothrond, stands under the same doom; and its end fulfills yet another prophecy. When Nargothrond is completed, Finrod calls a feast attended by Galadriel and the sons of Finarfin. When Galadriel has occasion to ask Finrod why he has no wife, "foresight came upon Fela-

gund as she spoke, and he said: 'An oath I too sha
must be free to fulfill it, and go into darkness. Nor
thing of my realm endure that a son should inherit' " (p
His prophecy helps structure the stories of Beren and T
it begins fulfillment in the Fourth Battle, Dagor Bragollac
when Finrod, cut off from his people and facing death in the
Fen of Serech, is rescued by Barahir, father of Beren. In thanks,
Finrod "swore an oath of abiding friendship and aid in every
need to Barahir and all his kin, and in token of his vow he gave
to Barahir his ring" (p. 152). This ring will later bring Beren
the help of Finrod, aid that will cause Felagund's death but in
the long run the furtherance of the destruction of Morgoth.
Moreover, the great-grandson of Beren's uncle Bregolas, Túrin
Turambar, will oversee, or rather find his fate enmeshed with,
the fulfillment of the second part of Finrod's prophecy. Again,
a look at the genealogy will clarify this part of the tale, for the
story of Túrin is not directly related to that of the Silmarils, but
his lineage is, as is his fate: "for it is woven with the fate of the
Silmarils and of the Elves; and it is called the Tale of Grief"
(p. 199). The brothers Huor and Húrin fought with great
honor in the Fifth Battle, Nirnaeth Arnoediad, and just before
its doleful end they speak prophetic words. Húrin tries to con-
vince Turgon to flee the battle and save his life. Huor speaks
more specifically and prophetically: "Out of your house shall
come the hope of Elves and Men. This I say to you lord, with
the eyes of death . . . from you and me a new star shall arise"
(p. 194). Huor predicts correctly; his son Tuor will wed Turgon's daughter Idril, who will bear Eärendil. Huor's brother
Húrin will, in the meantime, become father to Túrin, who in
time will travel to Nargothrond, led by Gwindor, lately escaped
from the mines of Morgoth. When Orodreth, successor to
Finrod in Norgothrond, learns of Túrin's parentage, he will
treat him with great honor and listen, disastrously, to his advice.
Túrin is young, ambitious, a mighty warrior, unlikely to heed

prudent counsel, and when a message arrives from Ulmo advising Nargothrond to shut its gates upon the world and cast down its bridge across Narog (built by Túrin's own counsel), Túrin resists and the bridge stays up, to the bane of the city. Thus the doom of Nargothrond results, on one side, from the creative ambition of Túrin. But the dark side of its doom comes from Morgoth. Because of Húrin's help to Turgon at Nirnaeth Arnoediad, Morgoth especially hates the father of Túrin. When Húrin is captured near the end of the battle (from which Turgon had escaped following the advice of Huor and Húrin) he is carried to Morgoth, but "Húrin defied him and mocked him. Then Morgoth cursed Húrin and Morwen and their offspring, and set a doom upon them of darkness and sorrow" (p. 197). Later when Morgoth learns that Agarwaen the son of Úmarth is in fact Túrin son of Húrin, he sends Glaurung to destroy, with his evil, the young man and his sister. But in so doing Glaurung meets his death, leaving Nargothrond ruined and unguarded, so that Húrin later enters it and finds the Nauglamír, which he will cast at the feet of Thingol in scornful payment for what he takes to be the careless and thoughtless treatment of his wife and daughter. The dwarves of Nogrod lay claim to the necklace (soon enriched by the Silmaril of Beren) as their own, killing Thingol for it and being killed in their turn by Beren, who passes the Silmaril on to his son Dior and then Dior's daughter Elwing, wife of Eärendil, to whom the Silmaril would not have otherwise come (nor the doom of Morgoth), had not Morgoth laid his curse upon Húrin and his family: the Second Law works with a vengeance, tying together the fates of Túrin, Nargothrond, and Thingol.

Thingol's is the second of the great fortress-kingdoms of Beleriand to fall, drawn into the Doom of Mandos by its king's desire for a Silmaril. I have already discussed the story of Thingol, Beren, and Lúthien, but not the reasons for its structure, which stem from the workings of the laws of Arda. In accordance with the Second Law, Melian foresees that a man (the as-yet unborn Beren) will be the first to break the Girdle around Doriath, "for doom greater than my power shall send him" (p. 144). That doom is of course a part of the First Law, the power of Ilúvatar's providence to destroy Morgoth and bring good from his evil. Beren will be the agent of that doom, and fate indeed seems the major force behind his success. Morgoth has pursued Beren's father to the death, until he has but twelve companions left. Through a typical evil ruse (the deception of Gorlim into revealing Barahir's hiding place) Morgoth succeeds in destroying Beren's father, but not the son, who was away "on a perilous errand." Beren dreams of the treachery and returns to find his father's body, and "swore upon it an oath of vengeance" against Morgoth. Pursuing the orcs who had slain Barahir and taken the ring given him by Finrod, he kills their captain, recaptures the ring, and escapes, "being defended by fate" (pp. 163–4). He then flees southward, entering Doriath and passing the previously impenetrable Girdle, even as Melian had foretold, for a "great doom lay upon him." Beren next falls under the influence of the Fourth Law, the enchantment of beauty, when he sees Lúthien in Neldoreth. Their love, clearly predestined, grows deep and strong, so that "in his fate Lúthien was caught," for "doom fell upon her" when she saw him (p. 165). All this means that Beren's career is part of the plan of Ilúvatar. Beren must capture the Silmaril so that it might ultimately pass to Eärendil and grant him entry to Valinor. But the quest for the Silmaril is of course Thingol's idea, and when he demands a jewel from Morgoth's crown as a bride-price for Lúthien, "he wrought the doom of Doriath, and was ensnared within the curse of Mandos" (p. 167); for as Finrod later declares, the Silmarils are "cursed with an oath of hatred, and he that even names them in desire moves a great power from slumber" (p. 169).

Even lesser elements of this tale stem from the effects of the laws of Tolkien's Secondary World. Two of Fëanor's sons, Celegorm and Curufin, have come to Nargothrond seeking refuge with Finrod, bringing with them what proves to be necessary to the success of Beren's quest, Huan and the knife Angrist, the help of which, however, will come only as a result of Fëanor's sons' evil action. Celegorm, lusting for Lúthien and the power marriage to her would bring, deceives and entraps her, but his dog Huan loves her selflessly (dog and elf show the two faces of the third law), helping her to escape and accompanying her. The brothers pursue, but Lúthien has rejoined Beren, who with the help of Huan staves off their attack and captures Curufin's knife Angrist, which could cut iron "as if it were green wood" (p. 177). Later Huan slays Carcharoth, who has swallowed the Silmaril with Beren's hand, after Beren had cut the jewel from Morgoth's crown.

The last of the fortress-kingdoms of the elves to fall is Gondolin, the one most eagerly sought and deeply hated by Morgoth, for he "feared Turgon ... foreboding that in some time that yet lay hidden, from Turgon ruin should come to him" (p. 196). Morgoth's prophetic fear parallels Huor's prophecy quoted above, that from Turgon and Huor a new star should arise. As potential grandfather to Eärendil, Turgon does indeed offer a grave threat to the evil one.

As is usual in *Quenta Silmarillion* the mechanism for the fulfillment of Morgoth's foreboding is the working out of his own evil intentions to good results (First Law), combined with the good results of the beneficent intentions of others. Ulmo has already predicted the coming end of Gondolin, declaring that though it would stand against Morgoth "longest of all the realms of the Eldalië," it too lies under the Doom of Mandos, so that Turgon may well find "treason awake within thy walls." But before this happens, Ulmo prophesies, "one shall come to warn thee, and from him beyond ruin and fire hope shall be born for Elves and Men." Ulmo therefore warns Turgon, "love not too well the work of thy hands," but remember rather that the "hope of the Noldor lieth in the West" (pp. 125–6). Ulmo's prophecy is in two parts, one of Maeglin, one of Tuor. Maeglin has his own chapter in *Quenta Silmarillion*, for evil as was his treason, without it the Silmaril of Beren would never have come to Valinor with Eärendil. Maeglin's story starts with Aredhel his mother, sister of Turgon in Gondolin, who desires leave to visit the sons of Fëanor, her friends of old. Turgon begrudgingly grants it, but on her journey she becomes entrapped in the forest of Nan Elmoth by the power of Eöl the Dark Elf, who has become enchanted by her beauty. They marry, though nowhere is their union described as love, but only as the product of the "enchantments" of Eöl. Maeglin is born, and after years of isolation, Aredhel grows weary of her life in the dark forest, desiring to see her brother again in Gondolin. Her son too wishes freedom to satisfy his ambitions. So they flee, pursued by the angry Eöl, who thus finds his forbidden way into the Hidden Kingdom. But Curufin has already warned Eöl not to "pursue those who love you no more," for such greed of possession will end in his death (p. 136). The prophecy comes true; for in Gondolin before the judgment seat of Turgon, Eöl in his wrath at his son's supposed disloyalty kills Aredhel who has stepped in front of Maeglin to save him from his father's spear. Turgon executes him for the slaying, but before he dies, Eöl prophesies that Maeglin will suffer the same fate, to be cast over the cliffs of the Encircling Mountains: "Here shall you fail of all your hopes, and here may you yet die the same death as I" (p. 138).

Eöl's prophecy begins coming true when Maeglin finds he loves his cousin Idril, daughter of Turgon, knowing all the while that he "desired her without hope. [For] The Eldar wedded not with kin so near." Idril finds his love for her shocking, "a crooked thing," as do the rest of the Gondolindrim, regarding it an "evil fruit of the Kinslaying, whereby the shadow of the curse of Mandos fell upon the last hope of the Noldor." Maeglin's thwarted love festered, turning gradually to "darkness in his heart," and preparing him for his fatal treachery (p. 139).

The positive half of Ulmo's prophecy regards Tuor, cousin of Túrin and the object of Huor's dying prophecy, who is chosen as the "instrument" of Ulmo's designs (p. 244). The Vala of the waters shows him the shield, sword, hauberk, and helm left in Nevrast by Turgon according to prophetic instructions, and leads him to the Hidden Kingdom. Tuor warns Turgon (as Ulmo had warned Orodreth) that as the curse of Mandos now nears fulfillment he had best abandon Gondolin, but Turgon listens instead to the ambitious counsel of Maeglin, as Orodreth had heeded Túrin. But Turgon at least remembers the prophecy of Huor and the identifying weapons of Tuor, and so allows him to marry Idril, thus making Maeglin's "secret hatred ... greater" (p. 245). Idril's spirit forebodes the same evil Ulmo had predicted, so she builds a secret exit from Gondolin, and just in time, for Maeglin, captured by orcs, reveals to Morgoth the secret of the Hidden Kingdom, and is promised Idril as his reward. Gondolin falls as a consequence of Maeglin's treachery, but he dies, as Eöl had prophesied, the same death as his father, cast over the cliff of Amon Gwareth by Tuor in the battle (p. 243). Seven-year-old Eärendil, son of Tuor and Idril, is carried by his mother to safety unknown by Morgoth, who thought that with Gondolin destroyed, "his triumph was fulfilled, recking little of the sons of Fëanor, and of their oath" (p. 244). Even in his victory, Morgoth's end approaches, for Eärendil is carried to the seacoasts, where he will later meet and marry Elwing, heir to the Silmaril of Beren.

Eärendil's voyage and its results are predicted just after the fall of Gondolin. When that disaster has apparently ended the hope of the Noldor and concluded the triumph of Morgoth, Ulmo goes to Valinor to speak of the need of the elves. "But Manwë moved not . . . The wise have said that the hour was not yet come, and that only one speaking in person for the cause of both Elves and Men, pleading for pardon on their misdeeds and pity on their woes, might move the counsels of the Powers" (p. 244). This is Eärendil; but how is he to get there? Again he succeeds by the indirect working of the Oath of Fëanor. Maedhros and his brothers, learning at last that Elwing yet lives and possesses the Silmaril, attack her people and destroy the realm of Eärendil, but fail to capture Elwing, who casts herself into the sea with the Silmaril upon her breast (p. 247). Ulmo helps her reach her husband, who perceives "no hope left in the lands of Middle-earth" and decides to try once again to reach Valinor, for he had long desired to find the "last shore, and bring ere he died the message of Elves and Men to the Valar in the West, that should move their hearts to pity" (p. 246). This time he succeeds, and "the wise have said that it was by reason of the power of the holy jewel" that he came to the Undying Lands (p. 248). Eärendil perceives that it is "my fate to bear" the Silmaril and his message to the Valar, a message welcomed and heeded at last by the Powers: "Pardon he asked . . . and mercy upon Men and Elves and succour in their need. And his prayer was granted" (p. 249).

Tolkien comes at last to the ending of his long tale, one overseen, he insists, by divine intentions, yet one filled with woe as well as wonder. With the eternal binding of Morgoth and the dispersal of the Silmarils in earth, sea, and sky, ends the tale in which, as Manwë declares, "beauty not before conceived [was] brought into Eä, and evil yet [was] good to have been." Tolkien bids his readers remember, however, the answer of Mandos: "And yet remain evil" (p. 98). That ambiguous beginning of the story of the Silmarils echoes its ending: "the lies that Melkor . . . sowed in the hearts of Elves and Men are a seed that does not die and cannot be destroyed; and ever and anon it sprouts anew, and will bear dark fruit even unto the latest days." If ever that "Marring" will be amended, "Manwë and Varda may know; but they have not revealed it" (p. 255).

IV

Reading *Akallabêth*

ঽ৶

AKALLABÊTH began as a dream, Tolkien's own subconscious voyage into an archetype, the Atlantis legend. Since childhood he had been disturbed by a recurrent nightmare, which he called his "Atlantis-haunting": "the dreadful dream of the ineluctable Wave, either coming up out of a quiet sea, or coming in towering over the green inlands," engulfing and sweeping away him and all his world (Carpenter, p. 170).

But the writing of *Akallabêth* involved Tolkien in one of his favorite literary tricks, the creation of the "real" source or origin of a famous tale. He did this for pure fun in *The Adventures of Tom Bombadil*, poems written, some of them, as early as the nineteen-twenties. Such works in this collection as "Fastitocalon" and "The Man in the Moon Stayed up too Late" stand, Tolkien implies with tongue firmly implanted in cheek, as the ultimate sources of the ancient Greek *Physiologus* and the English nursery rhyme "Hey Diddle Diddle" (see *Tolkien's World*, Chapter VII). He does the same in *Akallabêth*, though without intending humor. The land that sank, says Tolkien, was no longer spoken of by its old names Elenna, Andor, or Nú-menórë; men spoke thereafter of "Mar-nu-Falmar that was whelmed in the waves, Akallabêth the downfallen, Atalantë in the Eldarin tongue" (p. 281): thus Tolkien's mock-scholarly contribution to philology and literary history. "Real" or Primary World historical philology tells us that "Atlantis" comes from the name of Atlas, the Titan in Greek mythology who supports the heavens on his shoulders; the Atlas mountains in northwest Africa, lying near the Atlantic adjacent to the area where the island once supposedly stood, bear his name, one stemming, say historical linguists, from the Greek *tlénai*, "to bear or carry." Tolkien, however, provides the "real" origin of the word, one far more ancient than the Greek: "Atlantis" comes in fact, he implies, from *Atalantë*, the Quenya equivalent to the Númenórean *Akallabêth*, "the Downfallen" (p. 281) — not "that which supports" but "that which is fallen." With this reversal of meaning Tolkien sets up one of the major themes of *Akallabêth*: the significance of the Fall of Man.

The story of the sunken island civilization also lies much deeper in history, says Tolkien, than Plato's tale in the *Timaeus*. In this Greek work, Socrates' friend Critias tells an ancient Egyptian story of

> a mighty power which unprovoked made an expedition against the whole of Europe and Asia, and to which your city [Athens] put an end. This power came forth out of the Atlantic Ocean, for in those days the Atlantic was navigable; and there was an island situated in front of the straits which are by you called the pillars of Heracles; the island was larger than Libya and Asia put together... Now in this island of Atlantis there was a great and wonderful empire... This vast power, gathered into one, endeavoured to subdue at a blow our country and yours and the whole region within the straits.

Athens, however, supported by its goddess Athena, opposed and defeated the invasion:

> But afterwards there occurred violent earthquakes and floods; and in a single day and night of misfortune all your warlike men in a body sank into the earth, and the island of Atlantis in like manner disappeared in the depths of the sea.[1]

According to Plato, this story was first told to Solon (who died c. 559 B.C.) by the priests of the city of Sais in the Nile delta, who believed that the sinking of Atlantis happened some time after the founding of Athens, an event which by their reckoning occurred nine thousand years previously.[2] Tolkien, however, is rather more precise in *his* dating of the sinking of Atalantë: it happened in the year 3319 of the Second Age of Middle-earth, 3040 years before the War of the Rings at the end of the Third Age (see Appendix B of *The Return of the King*). He thus supplies a more "precise" date, a more "accurate" etymology, and a more "complete" version of the story of the island, its name, and its sinking.

But of course *Akallabêth* is more than mock-scholarly historical and philological research; it is Tolkien's first full-scale brief epic of men as opposed to elves, presenting his deepest thinking about death, the Gift of Men. Already in *Quenta Silmarillion* he had prepared for this tale, there presenting his profound understanding of the nature of human mortality. Men, he says, are unlike the deathless elves, who are bound forever to the life of the world; for Ilúvatar "willed that the hearts of Men should seek beyond the world and should find no rest therein; but they should have a virtue to shape their life, amid the powers and chances of the world, beyond the Music of the Ainur, which is as fate to all things else" (p. 41). But men must pay a price for this freedom of will and ability to yearn toward Ilúvatar: though their longings be immortal, their bodies are not:

> It is one with this gift of freedom that the children of Men dwell only a short space in the world alive, and are not bound to it, and depart soon whither the Elves know not. Whereas the Elves remain until the end of days... But the sons of Men die indeed, and leave the world; wherefore they are called the Guests, or the Strangers. Death is their fate, the gift of Ilúvatar, which as Time

wears even the Powers shall envy. But Melkor has cast his shadow upon it, and confounded it with darkness, and brought forth evil out of good, and fear out of hope. Yet of old the Valar declared to the Elves in Valinor that Men shall join in the Second Music of the Ainur (p. 42).

Here, in the first chapter of *Quenta Silmarillion*, Tolkien sets a major theme of *Akallabêth*, showing as well his grasp of human psychology. Always to yearn for what we do not have, to seek beyond the confines of our world, is our destiny, and one resulting directly from our freedom. Because of this combination of desire and liberty, unique in the mortal creatures of Arda, man is peculiarly susceptible to temptation, and in a way rather different from the liability of the elves; they long for what a member of their race once lost, the Silmarils, but men long for what they can never have, immortality in the flesh.

Tolkien thus uses Plato's story of Atlantis, but deepens its themes. The Atlanteans desired conquest and empire, and it appears that the punishment for their overreaching came from Athena, goddess of her eponymic city of Athens. The Númenóreans desired not merely conquest — though that was indeed one of their aims — they wanted an attribute of divinity itself, eternity. They wanted to be as gods — knowing not good and evil only, but endlessness — for Tolkien has blended Plato's legend of Atlantis with the Bible's story of the Fall of Man, to produce a tale of great resonance.

The Silmarillion as a whole presents three great Falls: of Morgoth, of the Elves, and of Men. Already in the First Age, Arda is postlapsarian, for a major theme in all of Tolkien's writings is the myth of the eternal return of the demonic: "Always after a defeat and a respite, the Shadow takes another shape and grows again" (I, 81–82). That theme finds statement in *Akallabêth* with Tolkien's first hint of the resurgence of Sauron after the defeat of Morgoth:

Manwë put forth Morgoth and shut him beyond the
World in the Void that is without ... Yet the seeds that
he had planted still grew and sprouted, bearing evil fruit,
if any would tend them. For his will remained and
guided his servants (p. 260).

This we learn even before the establishment of Andor,
the Land of Gift, as a reward for the Edain's help in the defeat
of Morgoth, a land rich and fair, whose inhabitants "knew no
sickness" (p. 261) — a second Eden, though with a serpent built
in:

But they did not thus escape from the doom of death
that Ilúvatar had set upon all Mankind, and they were
mortal still, though their years were long (p. 261).

A new star indexed, like Christ, the Land of Gift:

the Star of Eärendil shone bright in the West as a token
that all was made ready, and as a guide over the sea; and
... the Edain set sail upon the deep waters, following the
Star (p. 260).

Like Eden Andor has its prohibition: its people must not sail
westward toward Avallónë or Valinor, for

The design of Manwë was that the Númenóreans should
not be tempted to seek for the Blessed Realm, nor desire
to overpass the limits set to their bliss, becoming enam-
oured of the immortality of the Valar and the Eldar and
the lands where all things endure (p. 262).

With this Tolkien has achieved the depth and complexity of the
same kind of paradox animating and enriching the story of the
Fall in Genesis: the very act that would most mature the humanity of the first couple — learning the knowledge of good
and evil — is the only act forbidden them. Tolkien has, that
is, grasped one of the central facts of the inner life of man:

every act of human advancement is accompanied by, or bound up with, overreaching and guilt. In Andor, the very act most basic to the humanity instilled by Ilúvatar — "to seek beyond the World and ... find no rest therein" — is the act forbidden them by Manwë. For Manwë's "design" that the Númenóreans should not be tempted to seek for the Blessed Realm is of course the very thing that tempts them most. Milton too sensed this paradox; as his Eve says to the tree,

> [God] Forbids us then to taste; but his forbidding
> Commends thee more (IX, 752-3).

Manwë's prohibition likewise rankles against the very nature of man: "Eastward they must sail, but ever west their hearts returned":

> Now this yearning grew ever greater with the years; and the Númenóreans began to hunger for the undying city ... and the desire of everlasting life, to escape from death and the ending of delight, grew strong upon them (p. 263).

Thus Númenor found itself caught in an insoluble dilemma: created to yearn for the beyond, but forbidden to fulfill that yearning. In dealing creatively with this dilemma, Tolkien lifts *Akallabêth* in the direction of *Paradise Lost* with its implied solution of Milton's version of the same dilemma. Milton's God knows even before creating man that he will succumb to the temptation of knowing good and evil, for it is his nature that he should desire to know, a nature deliberately instilled in him by his Creator; thus Milton implies, though with great delicacy and indirection, that the Fall of Man was a good thing, allowing as it did for events even greater than Creation: Incarnation and Redemption. *O felix culpa!* [3] This Christian theme of the Fortunate Fall finds similar expression in Tolkien's work; man's dying and his yearning for everlasting life is part of Ilúvatar's

Grand Scheme, a plan to be revealed, ultimately, to men not to elves, who must remain forever of the earth, earthly. Man's yearning beyond the world is clear sign of a different destiny for him; as Manwë's messengers say to the Númenóreans:

> the mind of Ilúvatar concerning you is not known to the Valar, and he has not revealed all things that are to come. But this we hold to be true, that your home is not here, neither in the land of Aman nor anywhere within the Circles of the World.

How this is, and what it will mean, the Valar, even Manwë, do not know. At this point, Tolkien has the messengers speak a veiled prophecy of Christ, the ultimate solution, in Tolkien's view, for man's yearnings:

> Hope rather that in the end even the least of your desires shall have fruit. The love of Arda was set in your hearts by Ilúvatar, and he does not plant to no purpose. Nonetheless, many ages of Men unborn may pass ere that purpose is made known; and to you it will be revealed and not to the Valar (p. 265).

"To you it will be revealed"; humanity will be the agent and object of Redemption, and though Númenor sink, the love of Arda will be fulfilled.

Having thus established a context for his version of the Fortunate Fall, Tolkien can continue his tale as an evident revision of the biblical story. The Númenóreans have their paradise, but they remain dissatisfied, wanting what is forbidden them. Inevitably, the Shadow having risen in their hearts, the serpent enters their garden, in the form of Sauron, servant of Morgoth. Brought to Númenor apparently against his will — "yet in his secret heart he received it gladly, for it chimed indeed with his desire" (p. 271) — Sauron insinuated himself into the confidence of Ar-Pharazôn, king of Númenor, turning him to the worship of Morgoth and enmity for the Valar. When Ar-Pharazôn grows old and nears the death he dreads, there comes Sauron's great opportunity, the "hour [he] had prepared and long had awaited." He tempts the king with a version of the same hook that snared Eve: that the prohibition stands not for your own good but because the Forbidder wishes to keep you lesser than he:

> The Valar have possessed themselves of the land where there is no death; and they lie to you concerning it, hiding it as best they may, because of their avarice, and their fear lest the Kings of Men should wrest from them the deathless realm and rule the world in their stead (p. 274).

Or as Genesis puts it:

> And the serpent said unto the woman, ye shall not surely die: For God knows that in the day ye eat thereof, then your eyes shall be opened, and ye shall be as gods, knowing good and evil (Genesis 3:4–5).

Deluded, Ar-Pharazôn sails to the forbidden land, and like Adam, forever changes the world: "Númenor went down into the sea," "and the world was diminished, for Valinor and Eressëa were taken from it," so that "there is not now upon Earth any place abiding where the memory of a time without evil is preserved" (p. 279).

Just before recording this great punishment Tolkien gives a hint, as he has earlier, of the nature of the Redemption to come after many ages of men: it involves a willing self-sacrifice for others. Amandil, father of Isildur, one of the few remaining Faithful in Andor, attempts the same perilous journey undertaken by Eärendil, "to sail into the West," there to plead "for mercy upon Men and their deliverance from Sauron the deceiver." "And as for the Ban, I will suffer in myself the penalty"

(p. 275). But his effort fails, for "Man could not a second time be saved by any such embassy, and for the treason of Númenor there was no easy absolving" (p. 276). No journey "up," but a journey "down," Tolkien implies, an even greater absolution, must come in the distant future.

V

Three Silmarils, One Ring

&

HUMPHREY CARPENTER argues that "*The Lord of the Rings* was not so much a sequel to *The Hobbit* as a sequel to *The Silmarillion*" (p. 192). His assertion holds a deal of truth and I want to test it in this chapter, examining the relationships among the three works; but Carpenter misses two essential points: that *The Hobbit* stands in large part as a version for children of some portions of *The Silmarillion*, and that *The Lord of the Rings* is virtually an enlarged retelling of its predecessor *The Hobbit*. The three works, that is, show a rich and complicated inter-relationship, a development one from the other, not so simple as Carpenter suggests. But that Carpenter's argument is the version of the truth Tolkien himself wanted to believe is verified by his statement in the Foreword to the second edition of *The Lord of the Rings*; what is fascinating to note, however, is that the lapses of memory in this statement reveal that Tolkien *wants* it to be true that Frodo's story relates more closely to *The Silmarillion* than to Bilbo's, wants *his* version of the genesis of his three-volume masterpiece to prevail:

> This tale grew in the telling, until it became a history of the Great War of the Ring and included many glimpses of the yet more ancient history that preceded it. It was begun soon after *The Hobbit* was written and before its publication in 1937; but I did not go on with this sequel,

for I wished first to complete and set in order the mythology and legends of the Elder Days, which had then
been taking shape for some years.

This fascinating piece of misinformation stands as an early plug
for *The Silmarillion* (which is, Tolkien implies, an even more
important book than *The Lord of the Rings,* the work set aside
for his book about the Elder Days), but I think it more a fail-
ure of memory than a falsehood. We now know that *The Lord
of the Rings* was not begun until late December 1937, more
than two months *after* the publication of *The Hobbit.* The
reasons for Tolkien's lapse of memory become more clear as
the Foreword proceeds:

> I desired to do this [i.e., complete *The Silmarillion*] for
> my own satisfaction, and I had little hope that other
> people would be interested in this work, especially since
> it was primarily linguistic in inspiration and was begun
> in order to provide the necessary background of 'history'
> for Elvish tongues.
>
> When those whose advice and opinion I sought cor-
> rected *little hope* to *no hope,* I went back to the sequel,
> encouraged by requests from readers for more informa-
> tion concerning hobbits and their adventures.

This is Tolkien's version of the events of December 1937, when
Stanley Unwin, Tolkien's publisher, wrote suggesting that since
his first children's book was so immediately successful, a "large
public will be clamouring next year to hear more from you
about Hobbits!" (Carpenter, p. 182). But Tolkien had little desire, early in December 1937, to produce another book about
hobbits; he wanted to complete and publish *The Silmarillion,*
on which he had been laboring for twenty years and about
which he was almost pathetically eager for encouragement. In
the fall of that year he had given Unwin a large bundle of manuscripts of *The Silmarillion,* some in prose, some in verse; a

reader for Unwin had been, according to Carpenter, "very rude" in his comments about the rhyming couplets of "The Gest of Beren and Lúthien," but had found the prose version of the tale "enthralling." Unwin wrote to give Tolkien a decision about the manuscripts on December 15, telling him that though *The Silmarillion* "contains plenty of wonderful material" (he discreetly failed to mention the reader's response to the verses), "What we badly need is another book with which to follow up our success with *The Hobbit* and alas! neither of these manuscripts (the poem and *The Silmarillion* itself) quite fits the bill. I still hope that you will be inspired to write another book about the Hobbit" (Carpenter, p. 184). Tolkien's response on the next day shows his eagerness for encouragement about *The Silmarillion* and his uncertainty about the value of any more on hobbits: "My chief joy comes from learning that *The Silmarillion* is not rejected with scorn" (of course the poetic version of part of it *had* been, though he did not know this). "I have suffered a sense of fear and bereavement, quite ridiculous," says Tolkien, since sending off the manuscript to Unwin, "and I think if it had seemed to you to be nonsense I should have felt really crushed" (Carpenter, p. 184). Tolkien seems under the erroneous impression that Unwin's reader had read and enjoyed all of *The Silmarillion*, but Carpenter makes clear that he examined only the prose and poetic versions of the tale of Beren and Lúthien, and that "There is no evidence that any other part of *The Silmarillion* was read." Apparently Tolkien was never disabused; indeed, how could Unwin have responded, other than he did, to such touching self-revelation about a work that a professional publisher's reader had just found — in the verse part — rubbish? Tolkien's letter continues:

> But I shall certainly now hope one day to be able, or be able to afford, to publish *The Silmarillion*! Your reader's comments afford me delight (Carpenter, p. 184).

Thus Tolkien's memory in the Foreword to the second edition of *The Lord of the Rings* that he was given *"no hope"* for *The Silmarillion* is as inaccurate as his memory of the date of the event. There is of course nothing unusual or sinister about a sixty-five-year-old man's inability to remember the precise date and sequence of events some thirty years in the past; what is interesting is that the lapses of memory fit a pattern, they are connected, linked to Tolkien's desire to believe a certain version of the story of the origins of *The Lord of the Rings*. We may see how this is so with another look at the Foreword:

> I went back to the sequel, encouraged by requests from readers for more information concerning hobbits and their adventures. But the story was drawn irresistibly towards the older world, and became an account, as it were, of its end and passing away before its beginning and middle had been told.

Tolkien wanted to believe, when he wrote the Foreword, that Unwin had discouraged him about continuing *The Silmarillion* and that he had as a consequence of the discouragement turned from his unfinished and (apparently) unpublishable work to an already-begun manuscript of *The Lord of the Rings*. He wanted to believe, after *The Lord of the Rings* had become a classic, that it was perceived from the beginning as a natural culmination and conclusion of the tale of Middle-earth begun in *The Silmarillion*; he wanted to play down the relationship between *The Lord of the Rings* and *The Hobbit*, and play up the relationship between *The Lord of the Rings* and *The Silmarillion*. But the apparent truth of the matter is that in December 1937, Tolkien felt (though with inadequate justification) *encouraged* about being able one day to publish *The Silmarillion*, and that he undertook a sequel to *The Hobbit*, at least initially, as a means of becoming able to afford to publish his work about the Elder Days. *The Lord of the Rings* is an afterthought, an acci-

dent of the success of *The Hobbit*, called into being by a parallel combination of Unwin's quite legitimate desire for profit and
Tolkien's desire to find a way to publish *The Silmarillion*, and
was by no means already under way when Unwin responded to
the manuscripts of the Beren and Lúthien story. Tolkien found
it easy to forget these facts when *The Lord of the Rings* became
what it did — his masterpiece.

The Foreword goes on to stress the indebtedness of *The
Lord of the Rings* to *The Silmarillion* and the almost incidental
role of *The Hobbit*:

> the story was drawn irresistibly towards the older world,
> and became an account, as it were, of its end and pass-
> ing away before its beginning and middle had been told.
> The process had begun in the writing of *The Hobbit*, in
> which there were already some references to the older
> matter: Elrond, Gondolin, the High-elves, and the orcs,
> as well as glimpses that had arisen unbidden of things
> higher or deeper or darker than its surface: Durin, Moria,
> Gandalf, the Necromancer, the Ring. The discovery of
> the significance of these glimpses and of their relation to
> the ancient histories revealed the Third Age and its cul-
> mination in the War of the Ring.
>   ... the composition of *The Lord of the Rings* went on
> at intervals during the years 1936 to 1949.

To date the beginning of writing *The Lord of the Rings* in
1936, a year or perhaps a year and a half before publication of
The Hobbit, works to place it more in the orbit of *The Silmarillion* and less in the frame and influence of his children's
story, weakening the sense of the mediating role *The Hobbit*
played in the origin of Frodo's story; and it needs to be stressed,
as Carpenter and Tolkien do not, that without *The Hobbit*
there would have been no *Lord of the Rings*, for the latter is
The Hobbit writ large. The plot line of Tolkien's story for
children is repeated, on a larger canvas, almost exactly, in a ver-

sion for grownups, as the *The Lord of the Rings*. Both works begin in festivity: the "Unexpected Party" of *The Hobbit*, the "Long-Expected Party" of the *Rings*. Each presents, after the party, a lengthy scene of initiating information: about Smaug and the treasure, about Sauron and the Ring. Both hobbits then decide, with some trepidation, to leave the Shire on a perilous quest, the first stage of which will end at Rivendell. Both hobbits acquire a blade from an underground trove early in their journey: Bilbo gets Sting from the Trolls' cave, Frodo the sword from the barrow, and both use their blades heroically not long after. Both leave Rivendell with Gandalf and other companions after a conference with Elrond, and both attempt to pass next through the Misty Mountains. In each case a storm thwarts their negotiating the pass, so both enter a cavern instead. Here both are attacked by orcs and encounter Gollum for the first time (Bilbo in the riddle game, Frodo when he hears Gollum's softly padding feet in Moria). During the orcs' attack in the cavern, both hobbits are separated from their companions, Bilbo from Gandalf and the dwarves, Frodo and the walkers from Gandalf after his battle with the Balrog. The hero in both must proceed without the help of the Wizard. In both books the initial sequence of adventures preparing the hobbit for his great climactic adventure ends with a trip down a river to the edge of the territory of the evil power whose defeat is the object of the tale. In each book the hero, to reach the final adventure, must cross the blasted land surrounding the center of evil, reach and ascend a mountain, enter it by a hole in its side, and so entering discover the one vulnerable spot in the defenses of the evil: Smaug's unprotected side, Sauron's dependence on the Ring. Following the success of the quest, both works present a purging of Middle-earth in a great battle, of Five Armies in the first, of Morannon Gate in the sequel, each climaxing with the arrival of a flight of eagles signaling the victory of the hero's side. At the height of the last battle, both hobbits are wounded

(Bilbo by a blow on the head, Frodo by Gollum's teeth), but awaken to news of complete victory, the joy of which is tempered in both books with the report of the death of a king who had redeemed his former ill deeds in a heroic charge against the enemy (Kings Thorin and Theoden). Finally, after full recognition of the heroes, each takes the long journey homeward, parting along the way with various friends. Reaching Hobbiton, both find they have been dispossessed in their absence and must exert themselves one last time to regain Bag End.

But despite the remarkable similarity of their plot lines, *The Hobbit* and *The Lord of the Rings* are obviously not the same book; the chief differences stem from the distinction between their intended audiences, children in one, adults in the other, and between their quests, the one a venal adventure for revenge and wealth, the other an effort to save a world threatened by slavery. *The Lord of the Rings* repeats the plot line of *The Hobbit,* but deepening its themes, enlarging its vision. In *Tolkien's World* I argued that the depth and complexity of *The Lord of the Rings* were the fruits of what Tolkien learned in writing *The Hobbit*; especially was this true, I thought, of the differences between the quests of the two works, the one a quest for revenge and personal wealth, the other a quest to renounce and destroy the symbol and source of world domination in order to bring about peace and harmony. Tolkien grasped the power of such renunciation when Bilbo gave up the Arkenstone, thus making possible, ultimately, Frodo's wish to give up the Ring. Such an argument still has validity, but its weakness lies in its ignorance of *The Silmarillion.* Readers of Tolkien did not know that he had already written, but not yet published, a book with the same adult tone and renunciatory theme as *The Lord of the Rings* (Beren's and Eärendil's quests to deliver up a Silmaril surely foreshadow Frodo's quest). So to this extent Carpenter and Tolkien are right in their statements quoted above. Yet we must not forget that there are no hobbits in

Quenta Silmarillion: it is very fine, but it lacks certain qualities, chief among them a humanizing sense of humor and a sense of developing personality among its characters. And *The Hobbit* also is very fine, but it too lacks certain qualities, among them a sense of grandeur, of overarching and underpinning history, of depth. Tolkien had learned to combine these elements of his imagination by the time he finished *The Hobbit*, his recasting of parts of *The Silmarillion* as a children's story. *The Lord of the Rings*, his recasting of *The Hobbit* on a larger canvas, then became possible (though he didn't fully realize this in 1937). And apparently he never recognized the extent to which *The Silmarillion* served as a source of *The Hobbit*. Tolkien's Foreword to *The Lord of the Rings* indicates only that *The Hobbit* contains "some references to the older matter" of *The Silmarillion*, such as Elrond, the orcs, and the Necromancer. He has forgotten, or more likely never understood, that more than merely containing references to the world of *The Silmarillion*, *The Hobbit* is in fact a retelling of parts of its story; in his desire, that is, to stress the relationship between the *Rings* and *The Silmarillion*, he greatly underplays the relationship between the "older matter" and his children's story. An evil power has stolen a great treasure from a good and creative being, whose presence and powers have until his loss enriched those about him. The stolen treasure's physical essence is compressed and crystallized carbon — diamond— but the physical loss appears puny beside the moral devastation wrought by the theft. The former owner's son (or sons) grow pathetically grasping and vindictive, willing to destroy even friends or kinsmen who might hinder their efforts to regain the treasure, forgetting that treasure is as nothing compared to loyalty and love. A bald summary of part of *The Silmarillion* — but look again, a bald summary of part of *The Hobbit* as well! *The Hobbit* could be called *The Silmarillion* writ small.

Not only the larger plot line of *The Hobbit*, but lesser

elements as well, found their origin in the earlier work. Beren and Finrod (hero and king) set out from Nargothrond with their ten companions on a quest to regain a stolen treasure, the Silmaril, just as Bilbo and Thorin (hero and king) set out from Hobbiton with their thirteen companions to regain a stolen treasure. "Beneath the Shadowy Mountains they [Beren and Finrod] came upon a company of Orcs, and slew them all in their camp by night" (p. 170), as Bilbo and his friends encounter a group of goblins under the Misty Mountains, slaying many of them, not least their king. Later, "Sauron, being filled with suspicion, sent forth many wolves into the Elf-lands" to investigate Beren and his companions (p. 172), just as the area east of the Misty Mountains becomes filled with wolves after the slaying of the Great Goblin. Beren and Lúthien encounter Sauron's wolves and must be rescued from the scene by a pair of giant eagles (p. 182), just as Bilbo and his friends must be rescued from the wolves who have them treed and scorching, a rescue again accomplished by eagles. Not only must Tolkien's heroes in the two works both face orcs, wolves, and eagles, they must also get through an enchanted forest guarded by giant spiders (Mirkwood, Doriath), face imprisonment by a very unsympathetic ruler (King of the Wood-elves, Sauron), and be rescued by an invisible helper (Lúthien, enshrouded by her hair; Tolkien changes this in *The Hobbit*, where the hero himself becomes invisible, rescuing his friends instead of being himself rescued). Then the hero and his companions must penetrate the center of evil, steal the treasure (Silmaril, Arkenstone), and flee. In both cases the hero, in an act of supreme generosity, but in the service of a greater good, gives away the precious jewel. And in both cases lust for that jewel is related to the death of the king who desires it (Thorin, Thingol).

How did it happen that so much of *The Silmarillion* came out of Tolkien again as *The Hobbit*? *The Silmarillion* was largely completed, at least in outline form, by 1924, but Tolkien felt no compulsion to finish it as the nineteen-twenties wore on. Indeed, rather than bring it to a halt, he set about rewriting it, and in verse. He cast the tale of Túrin Turambar in a version of the four-beat alliterative line he knew so well from the Anglo-Saxon poetry of *Beowulf*, and the story of Beren and Lúthien in rhymed couplets. It seemed almost, as Carpenter suggests, that Tolkien did not *want* to complete *The Silmarillion*, for then there would be no more creative work in that rich Secondary World for him to do (Carpenter, p. 107). Tolkien's own imagination later recognized this truth about itself, a recognition lying behind the writing of "Smith of Wootton Major" in the nineteen-fifties; in this work he presents his own unwillingness, in the person of Smith, to give up the joy of entering at will into his created world of Faery. The large and wondrous world of *The Silmarillion* both filled and enriched his imagination throughout the nineteen-twenties, and as his children, especially his third son Christopher, grew older, he began telling its stories to them as well. Carpenter recounts that on many evenings in the early thirties the elder Tolkien would regale his son with tales about the "elvish war against the black power," about Beren and Lúthien, the orcs and the Necromancer, and a "dreadful red-eyed wolf" who "tore the companions of Beren to pieces" (Carpenter, p. 169). Already by this time Tolkien had composed a number of poems for his children, one called "The Dragon's Visit," in which a great worm encounters the redoubtable Miss Biggins, another called "Glip," about a "slimy creature who lives beneath the floor of a cave and has pale luminous eyes" (Carpenter, p. 106). In these poems, Tolkien's childlike sense of humor combined with his rich imagination to create works obviously appealing to children and obviously prophetic of *The Hobbit*. Perhaps it was inevitable that the world of *The Silmarillion* would one day creep into these stories and form *The Hobbit*, but it was an intrusion and a growth that would have to wait until Tolkien's invention of a character suitable for carrying the weight of the narrative of the earlier story in a manner appealing to children. That character is of course Bilbo Baggins, who was already beginning to be faintly apparent in Miss Biggins. As had so often happened in the writing of *The Silmarillion*, Tolkien's creativity flowered when literary experience (something already written down) confronted and was quickened by personal experience; in this case, Tolkien needed only to discover and explore that part of himself which could link his delight in telling stories to children with the part which delighted in creating mythology. The link was the hobbit himself, as much a part of his own character as the Beren who loved Edith/Lúthien:

> I am in fact a hobbit [he declared later in his life] in all but size. I like gardens, trees, and unmechanized farmlands; I smoke a pipe, and like good plain food (unrefrigerated), but detest French cooking; I like, and even dare to wear in these dull days, ornamental waistcoats. I am fond of mushrooms (out of a field); have a very simple sense of humour ... I go to bed late and get up late (when' possible). I do not travel much (Carpenter, p. 176).

And as Carpenter points out, Tolkien needed only to reflect on his own ancestry in order to contrive Bilbo's: as he was the son of the "enterprising" Mabel Suffield, one of the three daughters of John Suffield, who lived to extreme old age, so Bilbo likewise was the son of the unhobbitlike Belladonna Took, one of the three daughters of the Old Took, who also lived to extreme old age (Carpenter, p. 175).

Soon, therefore, after 1930 (it seems in retrospect predestined), Miss Biggins combined with Tolkien's own sense of himself to form Bilbo Baggins, who had "whole rooms devoted to clothes" in bright colors, loved his pipe and disliked travel, and had dinner twice a day when he could get it.[2] Having found Bilbo in his own heart, Tolkien needed to contrive something for him to do, since "This is a story of how a Baggins had an adventure" (*Hobbit*, p. 10). The unpublished *Silmarillion* lay at hand, and Tolkien mined it, but through the eyes of Bilbo or from the child's point of view, the perspective of one three feet tall. If Bilbo is to be three feet, his companions must be larger, but not too much so, and the dwarves of *The Silmarillion* were just that: "hobbits are (or were) a little people, about half our height, and smaller than the bearded dwarves. Hobbits have no beards" (*Hobbit*, p. 10). Bilbo will be, that is, the youngest and most timid of the company. Indeed, Tolkien's letter to Stanley Unwin of December 16, 1937, says as much; after remarking somewhat ruefully that though others want hobbits "the Silmarils are in my heart," he goes on to declare that "goodness knows what will happen" with his efforts at a new hobbit:

> Mr Baggins began as a comic tale among conventional and inconsistent Grimm's fairy-tale dwarves, and got drawn into the edge of it [i.e., *The Silmarillion*] — so that even Sauron the terrible peeped over the edge. And what more can hobbits do? (Carpenter, p. 185).

They could, of course, do much more than he realized in 1937; but though he is wrong here, he is quite right that the world of the Silmarils peeped ominously over the edge of Bilbo's story, perhaps even to a greater extent than he knew. Those "Grimm's fairy-tale" dwarves, for example: Tolkien has for the moment forgotten that their ancestry stretches hundreds of years farther back than the nineteenth-century Brothers Grimm, indeed all the way back to the *Elder Edda*. The notion that dwarves were created at the very foundation of the world, before even the elves, let alone men (an important point in *The Silmarillion*) Tolkien borrowed from that ancient Norse work, and when, in writing *The Hobbit*, he wanted names for his dwarves, he re-

turned, as it were, imaginatively *through The Silmarillion* to
that source:

> Then sought the gods   their assembly seats,
> The holy ones,   and council held,
> To find who should raise   the race of Dwarfs
> Out of Brimir's blood   and the legs of Blain.
>
> There was Motsognir   the mightiest made
> Of all the dwarfs,   and Durin next;
> Many a likeness   of men they made,
> The dwarfs in the earth,   as Durin said.
>
> Nyi and Nithli,   Northri and Suthri,
> Austri and Vestri,   Althjof, Dvalin,
> Nar and Nain,   Niping, Dain,
> Bifor, Bofur,   Bombur, Nori,
> An and Onar,   Ai, Nyothvitnir,
>
> Vigg and Gandalf,   Vindalf, Thrain,
> Thekk and Thorin,   Thror, Vit and Lit . . .[1]

The list concludes with Fili, Kili, Gloin, Dori, and Ori. Examining this list, we can see that already, merely in the naming of
his dwarves, Tolkien was establishing a stance or point of view
for his children's story, viewing the dwarves of the *Edda* from
the three-foot-high perspective of a reader of *The Hobbit*,
picking names suitable for the tone of Bilbo's world; Ori, Dori,
Nori, Bifur, Bofur, and Bombur, for example, seem clearly more
apt as companions for Bilbo Baggins, merely by the sounds of
their names, than Althjof or Nyothvitnir. *The Silmarillion* and
its sources, as sources for *The Hobbit*, will be used extensively,
but quite selectively. Take the character of the dwarves in
Bilbo's story; they come directly from *The Silmarillion*, but
with a noticeable slant:

Aulë made the dwarves strong to endure ... stone-hard, stubborn, fast in friendship and in enmity, and they suffer toil and hunger and hurt of body more hardily than all other speaking peoples (*Silmarillion*, p. 44).

As apt a description of Thorin Oakenshield as of the dwarf-lord of Nogrod; but yet when we see Thorin in person, we realize that though his character has indeed all the elements of Aulë's dwarves, there is a notable addition, a comic pomposity altogether suitable to what Tolkien intends in *The Hobbit*:

We are met together in the house of our friend and fellow conspirator, this most excellent and audacious hobbit — may the hair on his toes never fall out! ... We are met to discuss our plans, our ways, means, policy and devices (*Hobbit*, p. 25).

Another characteristic of the dwarves in *The Silmarillion* becomes typical of those in *The Hobbit*, and in a way that will control the development of the children's story: "the gems of the Noldor they praised above all other wealth"; Thingol gave them many, and "one there was as great as a dove's egg, and its sheen was as starlight on the foam of the sea; Nimphelos it was named, and the chieftain of the Dwarves of Belegost prized it above a mountain of wealth" (p. 92). A mixture of stubbornness and love of gems and treasure becomes the ruling passion in the heart of Thorin Oakenshield, whose name is a combination of the Thorin and Eikenskjaldi of the *Edda*; as Thorin once says, "the Arkenstone of my father ... is worth more than a river of gold ... I will be avenged on anyone who finds it and withholds it" (*Hobbit*, p. 279). The greatest and most prized of dwarf treasures in *The Silmarillion* is the Nauglamír, the Necklace of the Dwarves, made for Finrod Felagund and his stronghold in Nargothrond. Tolkien transformed the story of the Nauglamír into a central plot strand in *The Hobbit* — the story of the Arkenstone — but with changes that were to bear much fruit in *The Lord of the Rings.*

Finrod lived long and happily in Nargothrond, pleasuring in his great treasure, "Nauglamír, the Necklace of the Dwarves, most renowned of their works in the Elder Days." But Finrod found himself bound by oath to help Beren, and in aiding that great hero he met his death in the dungeons of Sauron. Soon thereafter his city fell under attack by Morgoth and an army led by Glaurung, the Father of Dragons. Nargothrond overthrown, its inhabitants dead, Glaurung settled into the ruins in dragonlike fashion to enjoy its treasures: "he gathered all the hoard and riches of Felagund and heaped them, and lay upon them in the innermost hall, and rested a while" (p. 215). A dragon destroys a realm and its capital, and settles in upon its heaps of treasure — an element in *The Silmarillion* that becomes the background and reason for the story of *The Hobbit*: Smaug has destroyed the dwarf kingdom at the Lonely Mountain and settles in upon its heap of treasure, an act Thorin and his companions vow to revenge and so recapture their city. The heart of Nargothrond's treasure is Nauglamír, which figures in *The Silmarillion* in a way that provides for Tolkien the role of the Arkenstone, heart of the Lonely Mountain's treasure in *The Hobbit*. Some time after the fall of Nargothrond, Túrin Turambar kills the dragon Glaurung, leaving the ruins of Finrod's city unguarded, just as the heroic Bard kills Smaug, leaving the Lonely Mountain with no worm to watch it. Later Húrin finds the Nauglamír in Nargothrond and takes it to Thingol, a gift greatly displeasing to the dwarves of Nogrod, who feel that it is rightfully theirs since they made it. In like manner, Bilbo finds the Arkenstone and soon gives it to Bard and the elves opposing Thorin, much to the horror and wrath of the new King under the Mountain, who feels that it is rightfully his. Thingol and the dwarves quarrel over the necklace (which by this time is enriched by the mounting in it of the Silmaril cap-

tured by Beren), with the result that first Thingol, and later
the dwarves, are killed, even as Thorin quarrels with the men
and elves who hold the Arkenstone, an act followed (though
not as a consequence of the quarrel) by the deaths of both
Thorin and many of his former enemies in the Battle of Five
Armies.

So *The Hobbit* follows from *The Silmarillion*, as *The
Lord of the Rings* follows from *The Hobbit*, in a way that
neither Carpenter nor Tolkien himself seems to have realized.
But if *The Silmarillion* shrank into *The Hobbit*, which then
grew again into *The Lord of the Rings*, can we trace the linea-
ments of Tolkien's earliest work in his three-volume masterpiece? Is *The Lord of the Rings*, that is, really a sequel to *The
Silmarillion*? Indeed there is a sense in which Carpenter is correct in his assertion quoted at the beginning of this chapter; we
need only to add and remember that *The Hobbit* was the mid-
wife in this succession.

The most touching way *The Silmarillion* influenced *The
Lord of the Rings* through *The Hobbit* lies in the parallels
between the stories of Beren and Lúthien and Frodo and Sam;
human hero and elvish heroine become lone hobbits, dependent
upon each other's courage and love. Beren has been asked to
perform an impossible quest, quite beyond any mortal's power:
capture a Silmaril from Morgoth's crown. Frodo has been required to perform an equally hopeless quest: carry the Ring to
Mount Doom and destroy it. The one quest is to get something,
the other to get rid of something: lying between them is Bilbo's
great and heroic renunciation of the Arkenstone. Both Beren's
and Frodo's quests involve the hero's entering the realm of the
enemy (Morgoth, Sauron), from which there seems no hope of
escape. Soon before entering that realm, the hero attempts to
leave behind his companion (Lúthien, Sam) in order to spare
that dear friend from the terrible fate ahead, but in both cases
the companion catches up, determined to accompany the hero:

a clear growth over *The Hobbit*, in which the dwarves seriously consider whether they should abandon Bilbo in the goblin-tunnels under the Misty Mountains. Later on each hero is imprisoned; the companion, standing outside, not knowing what else to do, sings. Beren lies in the pits of Sauron, mourning Finrod:

> In that hour Lúthien came, and standing upon the bridge that led to Sauron's isle she sang a song that no walls of stone could hinder. Beren heard, and he thought that he dreamed ... And in answer he sang a song of challenge (p. 174).

Thousands of years later, in Middle-earth, Sam has followed the orcs and Frodo into Cirith Ungol, hoping to rescue his master. He enters but cannot find him, so "weary and feeling finally defeated," and "moved by what thought in his heart he could not tell, Sam began to sing ... He thought that he heard a faint voice answering him" (III, 226).

The companions rescue the heroes, and later, both wearing disguises of the evil realm, enter the enemy's land (Frodo and Sam dressed as orcs, Beren and Lúthien as a werewolf and a vampire). In both cases the fulfillment of the quest ends in the mutilation of the hero; Carcharoth bites off Beren's hand, Gollum, Frodo's finger. And in both cases, the two heroic pairs lie exhausted after their victories, facing certain death in the ensuing conflagration. But in both works, the eagles come to their rescue at the last moment:

> the quest of the Silmaril was like to have ended in ruin and despair; but in that hour above the wall of the valley three mighty birds appeared ... Then they lifted up Beren and Lúthien from the earth, and bore them aloft into the clouds. Below them suddenly thunder rolled, lightnings leaped upward, and the mountains quaked (p. 182).

And so it was that Gwaihir saw them with his keen far-
seeing eyes, as down the wild wind he came ... And in a
dream, not knowing what fate had befallen them, the
wanderers were lifted up and borne far away out of the
darkness and the fire (III, 229).

Standing between Thorondor's rescue of Beren and Lúthien and
his descendant Gwaihir's feat is of course the eagles' rescue of
Bilbo, Gandalf, and the dwarves from the flaming trees east of
the Misty Mountains; *The Hobbit*, that is, mediated the influence, a truth that holds throughout.

Afterword

Notes

Index

Afterword:
Unfinished Tales

AFTER I HAD PREPARED the final draft of this book for the press, I learned that Christopher Tolkien was about to release a new collection of his father's works under the title *Unfinished Tales.* That volume contains, among other things about the Three Ages, two versions of stories in *Quenta Silmarillion,* "Of Tuor and His Coming to Gondolin" and the *"Narn i Hîn Húrin,"* and accounts ancillary to *Akallabêth,* "A Description of the Island of Númenor" and "The Line of Elros: Kings of Númenor." Anyone interested, as I am, in the growth of *The Silmarillion* will want to study *Unfinished Tales,* not only for its intrinsic value but also because its relationship to the former provides what will become a classic example of a long-standing problem in literary criticism: what, really, *is* a literary work? Is it what the author intended (or may have intended) it to be, or is it what a later editor makes of it? The problem becomes especially intense for the practicing critic when, as happened with *The Silmarillion,* a writer dies before finishing his work and leaves more than one version of some of its parts, which then find publication elsewhere. Which version will the critic approach as the "real" story?

Unfortunately, there are no completely satisfactory answers to the most difficult critical problems; sometimes we can do little better than try to state the issue as clearly as possible. Christopher Tolkien has helped us in this instance by honestly pointing out that *The Silmarillion* in the shape that we have it is the invention of the son not the father. There is no "real" *Silmarillion*; it died as a dream and a plan in the mind of Tolkien:

> On my father's death it fell to me to try to bring the work into publishable form. It became clear to me that the attempt to present, within the covers of a single book, the diversity of the materials — to show *The Silmarillion* as in truth a continuing and evolving creation extending over more than half a century — would in fact lead only to confusion and the submerging of what is essential. I set myself therefore to work out a single text, selecting and arranging in such a way as seemed to me to produce the most coherent and internally self-consistent narrative. (pp. 8–9)

If the work was to be printed at all, the editor had to play his part; and we can only be grateful. But we always wonder, what might the original work have been like, and what was added or deleted by the editor? *Unfinished Tales* gives us occasion to consider these questions anew, while the Introduction to the volume presents Christopher Tolkien's own working solution to the problem of the "finished nature" of *The Silmarillion*. He admits frankly that *Unfinished Tales* may well "tend to contribute less to the history of the invented world itself than to the history of its invention." [1] In other words he makes no claim that these tales are anything *other* than unfinished, whereas, by editor's fiat, he makes a much larger claim for *The Silmarillion*, declaring that "I have indeed treated the published form of *The Silmarillion* as a fixed point of reference of the same order as the writings published by my father himself, without taking into account the innumerable 'unauthorised' decisions between variants and rival versions that went into its making." [2]

This forthright admission strikes me as a sensible way of treating *The Silmarillion,* and it is the way I have approached it in the present study — as a finished book surrounded by a nimbus of discarded or incomplete versions, some of which may have their own interest and published existence.

Indeed readers of *The Silmarillion* knew already that some volume like *Unfinished Tales* might someday appear. Christopher Tolkien assured us in his Foreword that there is "a wealth of unpublished writing by my father concerning the Three Ages, narrative, linguistic, historical, and philosophical, and I hope that it will prove possible to publish some of this at a later date" (p. 9). *Unfinished Tales* is the firstfruits of that wealth, and now we learn from its Introduction that we can hope for more: *The Book of Lost Tales* may be next. Tolkien's story of the Silmarils continues to grow.

Notes

ਵ੍ਹ

Introduction (pages ix–xiii)
1. Humphrey Carpenter, *Tolkien: A Biography* (Boston: Houghton Mifflin, 1977), p. 184.
2. J. R. R. Tolkien, *The Lord of the Rings* (Boston: Houghton Mifflin, 1965), I, 5. Future references to this work will be identified in the text by volume and page number.
3. Tolkien provides a translation for these lines in *The Road Goes Ever On* (Boston: Houghton Mifflin, 1967), p. 64.
4. J. R. R. Tolkien, "On Fairy-Stories," *Tree and Leaf* (Boston: Houghton Mifflin, 1965), pp. 52–53.

Chapter I (pages 1–20)
1. Carpenter, p. 172. Future references identified in the text.
2. *The Prose Edda of Snorri Sturluson*, trans. Jean I. Young (Berkeley: University of California Press, 1971), pp. 105–6.
3. Jakob Grimm, *Teutonic Mythology*, trans. James S. Stallybrass, 4 vols. (New York: Dover, 1966), I, 374.
4. Tolkien, "On Fairy-Stories," p. 42.
5. *The Kalevala*, trans. John Martin Crawford, 2 vols. (New York: John B. Alden, 1888), II, 543, 545.
6. J. R. R. Tolkien, *The Silmarillion* (Boston: Houghton Mifflin, 1977), p. 218. Future references will be identified in the text.
7. *The Poetic Edda*, trans. Henry Adams Bellows (London: Oxford University Press, 1923), p. 371.
8. *Ibid.*, p. 383.
9. *The Kalevala*, p. 561.
10. *The Ballad Book*, ed. MacEdward Leach (New York: Harper, 1955), pp. 131–2.
11. *The Mabinogion*, trans. Gwyn Jones and Thomas Jones (New York: Dutton, 1974), p. 96.

12. *Ibid.*, p. 111.
13. *Ibid.*, p. 113.
14. Erich Neumann, *The Origins and History of Consciousness* (New York: Pantheon, 1954), p. 195.
15. Tolkien, "On Fairy-Stories," p. 48.

CHAPTER II (pages 21–40)
1. "On Fairy-Stories," p. 54.
2. *Ibid.*, p. 55.
3. John Dryden, "Song for St. Cecilia's Day, 1687," in *The Works of John Dryden*, ed. Earl Miner *et al.* (Berkeley: University of California Press, 1971).
4. Plato, *The Republic*, X, 617, trans. Benjamin Jowett (Oxford: Clarendon, 1953). I am indebted to John Hollander, *The Untuning of the Sky: Ideas of Music in English Poetry, 1500–1700* (1961), for this and succeeding references in classical literature to music.
5. Aristotle, *On the Heavens*, trans. W. K. C. Guthrie (London: Loeb, 1939), II, ix.
6. Milton, *Second Prolusion, Complete Poems and Major Prose*, ed. Merrit Y. Hughes (New York: Odyssey Press, 1957), p. 604. All references to Milton are from this edition and will be identified in the text.
7. Cicero, *De Re Publica*, trans. C. W. Keyes (London: Loeb, 1928), pp. 271–3.
8. Milton, pp. 81–2.
9. "On Fairy-Stories," p. 71.
10. Clyde S. Kilby, *Tolkien and The Silmarillion* (Wheaton, Illinois: Harold Shaw, 1976), p. 59.
11. J. R. R. Tolkien, "*Beowulf*: The Monsters and the Critics," *An Anthology of Beowulf Criticism*, ed. Lewis E. Nicholson (University of Notre Dame Press, 1963), pp. 68, 71. Tolkien's lecture first appeared in the *Proceedings of the British Academy*, XXII (1936), 245–95.
12. *Ibid.*, p. 68.
13. *Ibid.*, p. 73.
14. "On Fairy-Stories," pp. 70–71.
15. *Ibid.*, p. 73.
16. Cynewulf, *Crist*, trans. Albert S. Cook (Boston: Ginn, 1900), p. 21.

CHAPTER III (pages 41–63)
1. *The Kalevala*, II, 615.
2. *Ibid.*, II, 732.

3. *Ibid.*, II, 679.
4. *Ibid.*, II, 696–7.
5. "On Fairy-Stories," p. 37.
6. Kilby, *Tolkien and The Silmarillion*, p. 56.
7. Goethe, *Faust*, trans. Louis Macneice (Oxford University Press, 1951), p. 41.

CHAPTER IV (pages 64–72)
1. *The Dialogues of Plato*, trans. Benjamin Jowett, 4 vols. (Oxford: Clarendon, 1953), III, 713.
2. *Ibid.*, III, 712.
3. "O happy sin!" For a fine discussion of the role of this concept in the history of western literature, see Arthur O. Lovejoy, "Milton and the Paradox of the Fortunate Fall," *Essays in the History of Ideas* (Baltimore: Johns Hopkins Press, 1948). Lovejoy quotes Gregory the Great: "certainly, unless Adam had sinned, it would not have behooved our Redeemer to take on our flesh. Almighty God saw beforehand that from that evil because of which men die, He would bring about a good which would overcome that evil" (p. 288). Milton expresses the idea with Adam's words:

"O Goodness infinite, Goodness immense,
That all this good of evil shall produce,
And evil turn to good — more wonderful
Than that which by creation first brought forth
Light out of darkness! Full of doubt I stand,
Whether I should repent me now of sin
By me done or occasioned, or rejoice
Much more that much more good thereof shall spring"
(XII, 469–76).

CHAPTER V (pages 73–90)
1. *The Elder Edda*, pp. 6–7.
2. J. R. R. Tolkien, *The Hobbit* (Boston: Houghton Mifflin, 1966), p. 9. Future references will be identified in the text.

AFTERWORD (pages 93–95)
1. J. R. R. Tolkien, *Unfinished Tales* (Boston: Houghton Mifflin, 1980), p. 3.
2. *Ibid.*, p. 3.

Index